Casserole Cooking
Myra Street

Casserole Cooking

Contents

First published in 1977 by Sundial Books Limited
59 Grosvenor Street, London W1

Ninth impression, 1980

© 1977 Hennerwood Publications Limited

ISBN 0 904230 43 0

Printed in England by Severn Valley Press Limited

Introduction

It is perhaps extraordinary to think that the words 'casserole' and 'stew' mean exactly the same, for they conjure up two entirely different concepts in most people's minds. One thinks of a casserole as being French and exotic, rich in flavour and served in an attractive dish. A stew on the other hand, brings to mind cheap cuts of meat which, cooked in any other way, might well be tough. Some of us possibly remember the Irish Stew of school meals as being uninteresting and tasteless, but there is no reason why it shouldn't be as flavoursome as any exciting French casserole.

The essence of casserole cooking is the relatively slow cooking of a mixture of ingredients and a small amount of liquid, in a dish which has a close fitting lid. The fit of the lid is important as it ensures the richness of the result and the minimal loss of liquid. Ideally, too, the casserole dish should distribute heat well and evenly, so that food doesn't stick on the bottom. This is why the enamelled cast iron casseroles are so popular. China, pottery, earthenware and heat resistance glass are all satisfactory, although much more fragile; and it is not a good thing to have any cracks in dishes as they not only harbour germs but often allow liquids to exude.

Nowadays the range and choice of casseroles are marvellous and can add enormously to the look of the table and the pleasure of eating. Before using a particular type of dish, check first that it is suitable for the method of cooking chosen. Some are not suitable for cooking on top of the cooker so care must be taken.

Mention should also be made of the slow cooking electric casseroles that are now marketed by several manufacturers. Do be careful to follow the maker's instructions and in particular note that some of these cookers must be pre-heated before any ingredients are put in, and the stock or liquid to be used should be brought to the boil before adding.

The two main advantages of these new cookers are that they are said to be economical, using little electricity, and they cook very slowly, which is useful if you are likely to be out all day. They are also good for the tougher cuts of meat which need very slow cooking, going back to the old fashioned principle of hay box cookery!

Whatever type of container you use, remember that casseroles are ideal for using in conjunction with automatic ovens, but it is advisable to add another quarter or half an hour to the cooking time in order to allow an electric oven to warm up. Gas cookers do not require preheating.

Cold start casserole

In nearly all the recipes given in this book, I have recommended that the meat to be casseroled should first be fried in butter or fat, as this gives a better looking and better tasting result. It is possible – and advisable if the meat is one of the tougher cuts, such as shin of beef – to cook the meat very slowly without frying first.

Freezing

Frozen meat must be thawed if the recipe states that the meat must first be browned. All poultry and game must be thawed before using in any type of cooked dish as harmful bacteria can lurk near the bone. If the flesh around the bone is still frozen when the bird is cooked, the heat may not penetrate fully and harmful bacteria will not be killed off by the high temperature but may even multiply in the warmth.

Cooked casseroles can be reheated directly from the frozen state and a quantity for 4 persons will take 1–1½ hours to reheat thoroughly at 160°C, 325°F, Gas Mark 3.

Packing casseroles for the freezer

Pyrosil containers can be used in the freezer and are suitable for using direct from freezer to oven. This also applies to foil containers and metal containers. However few of us have enough freezer space or enough casseroles to leave the meat in the containers. The best way is to freeze in the casserole, then turn out onto double thickness foil and seal well. Label each casserole with the contents and the description of the casserole and it can then be put back into the same casserole for reheating without any difficulty from awkward frozen shapes.

Casseroles flavoured with herbs, wine and spices, do tend to change flavour in the freezer. Over 3–4 weeks this is not too noticeable but over several months you may find that you have to adjust the flavourings when reheating. Undercook casseroles to be frozen by half an hour.

Cooking meat in bulk for casseroles pays dividends in time and kitchen mess. Several pounds of beef, lamb, pork or veal can be browned at one session, casseroled with chopped onions and seasoning for 1 hour then divided in 2, 4, 6 or 8 portions. Prepare vegetables and herbs and cook as for a freshly made casserole.

Cooking times for casseroles depend very much on the quality of meat used and to some

extent the casserole dish itself, so always test your casserole at the minimum time given to make sure the meat does not become overcooked.

Thickening and stock for casseroles

Casseroles are interesting and creative to make, as the flavour can always be varied to suit the mood of the cook. Basically meat or poultry, vegetables, herbs, seasoning and stock are the ingredients. A change of herb or vegetable can transform the basic brown stew or chicken casserole into an exciting meal to suit the individual tastes of each family. Thickening for a casserole is dependent on individual taste. Some people prefer thicker consistencies to others and the easiest way to deal with this is with 'beurre manié'. This is butter and flour kneaded together and used for thickening gravies. This method helps to give a glossy sauce and is I think more palatable than cornflour.

The stock used in the recipes can either be made as directed at the beginning of the beef, poultry or fish sections if time and ingredients are available. Alternatively stock cubes can be made up with water and used as directed. Remember though that these can be salty.

The following terms appear in the recipes and it is as well to understand their meaning.

Baste To spoon fat or liquid over food.

Beurre manié Kneaded butter and flour to form a mixture for thickening sauces, ragouts, stews and casseroles. Use 2 parts butter to 1 part flour and work into a paste. Add to the liquid in small pieces and whisk or stir well. Some people find it easier to add liquid to beurre manié, blend, and return to the main part of the sauce. Use 25 g (1 oz) butter, 15 g ($\frac{1}{2}$ oz) flour, 600 ml (1 pint) liquid.

Blanche To whiten or to plunge into cold water and bring to the boil. With green vegetables plunge into boiling water for 1 minute before cooking by another method.

Bouquet garni Consists of a collection of herbs in a small muslin bag. 1 Bay leaf, sprig of thyme, 3 parsley stalks. May be tied together and removed after cooking if muslin is not available.

Fry To cook over a brisk heat to obtain a good seal and a good colour.

Marinade To soak meat, poultry or game in oil, vinegar or wine and vegetables before cooking.

Roux Another important thickening agent made by melting butter in a saucepan and adding the flour to make a ball of dough which is known as the 'roux'. White roux is used for white sauces accompanying veal, chicken and fish dishes. Blond roux, where butter is browned slightly, is used for chicken and fish.
Brown roux is made by cooking flour in the fat until a rich brown colour is obtained. The hot liquid is then added gradually. Excellent for brown stews and dark sauces in casseroles.

Sauté To fry gently in fat for a golden result.

Sweat To cook vegetables or meat in a little fat over very low heat to avoid browning.

There are several points to look for when choosing beef, whether it is for the casserole, the roasting tin, frying pan or grill. Good beef is a deep red colour with a marbling of fat through it. It is this marbling which helps to give the beef its flavour and tenderness. Dark browny red, dried beef has been exposed to the air too long.

Suitable cuts of beef for the casserole: Leg of mutton cut, Brisket, Neck, Shin, Flank, Chuck steak, Leg of beef, Silverside.

Topside can be used for really special dishes.

To make Beef stock place 1–1½ kg (2–3 lb) of chopped beef bones, preferably with some marrow bone, in a saucepan with 3–6 pints water, 1 onion, 1 carrot, 1 small piece of turnip or celery, bouquet garni and some peppercorns. Bring to the boil and simmer until liquid is reduced by half. Strain and then remove fat when cool.

Alternatively make in a pressure cooker.

To freeze stock: Place in 300 ml (½ pint) or 600 ml (1 pint) boxes, freeze and pack in polythene bags in squares for easy storage. Small cubes may be frozen in ice trays and transferred to polythene bags when frozen.

Beefburgers with orange barbecue sauce

Metric

4 beefburgers
2 medium-sized onions,
peeled and sliced
1 × 15 ml spoon oil
15 g butter
1 × 5 ml spoon flour
150 ml orange juice
fresh or canned
1 × 5 ml spoon finely
grated orange rind
(optional)
½ teaspoon Worcestershire
sauce
1 × 15 ml spoon wine
vinegar
1 × 15 ml spoon tomato
purée
4 canned tomatoes,
drained
Salt and freshly ground
black pepper

Imperial

4 beefburgers
2 medium-sized onions,
peeled and sliced
1 tablespoon oil
½ oz butter
1 teaspoon flour
¼ pint orange juice
fresh or canned
1 teaspoon finely grated
orange rind (optional)
½ teaspoon Worcestershire
sauce
1 tablespoon wine vinegar
1 tablespoon tomato purée
4 canned tomatoes,
drained
Salt and freshly ground
black pepper

Cooking Time: 30 minutes
Oven: 160°C, 325°F, Gas Mark 3

Brown the beefburgers and sauté the onions gently in the oil. Place in a casserole. Make a roux with the butter and flour, add the orange juice, Worcestershire sauce, vinegar and tomato purée. Cook well, stir in tomatoes and season well. Pour into the casserole, cover and cook for 20 minutes. Taste and adjust the seasoning before serving. Decorate with blanched strips of orange rind, if liked. Serve with baked potatoes and a crisp green salad with slices or segments of orange.

Beef in beer

Metric

2 onions, peeled and diced
2 carrots, peeled and
sliced
50 g mushrooms, washed
and sliced
3 × 15 ml spoons oil
450 g braising steak,
cubed
1 × 15 ml spoon seasoned
flour
2 × 15 ml spoons tomato
purée
150 ml beer
Salt and freshly ground
black pepper
1 × 5 ml spoon thyme
1 bay leaf

To garnish:
Triangles of toast

Imperial

2 onions, peeled and diced
2 carrots, peeled and
sliced
2 oz mushrooms, washed
and sliced
3 tablespoons oil
1 lb braising steak, cubed
1 tablespoon seasoned
flour
2 tablespoons tomato
purée
¼ pint beer
Salt and freshly ground
black pepper
1 teaspoon thyme
1 bay leaf

To garnish:
Triangles of toast

Cooking Time: 1½–2 hours
Oven: 180°C, 350°F, Gas Mark 4

Sweat the vegetables in 2 × 15 ml spoons (2 tablespoons) oil for 5 minutes. Remove from heat and place into a casserole. Toss the meat in the flour and fry until brown over a brisk heat, adding the remaining oil. Place on top of the vegetables, pour over the tomato purée mixed with the beer, seasoning and herbs. Cook, covered, in the oven for 1½ hours. Remove the bay leaf, taste and adjust the seasoning. Garnish with triangles of toast.

Beef and lentil stew

Metric

2 × 15 ml spoons oil
450 g braising steak,
trimmed of fat and cut
into 2½ cm cubes
1 onion, peeled and diced
1 carrot, scraped and
diced
100 g lentils, soaked in
450 ml stock
Salt and freshly ground
black pepper
½ teaspoon mustard
½ teaspoon Worcestershire
sauce
396 g can tomatoes
½ teaspoon sweet basil
1 bay leaf
½ teaspoon sugar

Imperial

2 tablespoons oil
1 lb braising steak,
trimmed of fat and cut
into 1 inch cubes
1 onion, peeled and diced
1 carrot, scraped and
diced
4 oz lentils, soaked in
¾ pint stock
Salt and freshly ground
black pepper
½ teaspoon mustard
½ teaspoon Worcestershire
sauce
14 oz can tomatoes
½ teaspoon sweet basil
1 bay leaf
½ teaspoon sugar

Cooking Time: 1½ hours
Oven: 160°C, 325°F, Gas Mark 3

Heat the oil in a frying pan and fry meat until browned and
sealed. Transfer to casserole. Sauté vegetables until transparent and slightly browned, add to casserole. Add lentils
soaked in stock, seasoning, chopped tomatoes and juice,
herbs and sugar. Bring to just below boiling and pour over
the meat in the casserole. Cook, covered, for 1–1½ hours.
Remove bay leaf. Taste and adjust seasoning. Serve with a
crisp green vegetable.

Braised sliced beef

Metric

2 medium-sized carrots,
peeled and diced
1 small turnip, peeled and
diced
1 large onion, peeled and
diced
1 medium-sized parsnip,
peeled and diced
1 medium-sized leek, well
washed and sliced
1 clove garlic, crushed
3 × 15 ml spoons oil
700 g braising beef, cut
into 7½ cm × 5 cm slices
Bouquet garni
Salt and freshly ground
black pepper
600 ml stock
150 ml red wine
2 × 5 ml spoons
Worcestershire sauce

Imperial

2 medium-sized carrots,
peeled and diced
1 small turnip, peeled and
diced
1 large onion, peeled and
diced
1 medium-sized parsnip,
peeled and diced
1 medium-sized leek, well
washed and sliced
1 clove garlic, crushed
3 tablespoons oil
1½ lb braising beef, cut
into 3 inch × 2 inch
slices
Bouquet garni
Salt and freshly ground
black pepper
1 pint stock
¼ pint red wine
2 teaspoons Worcester-
shire sauce

Cooking Time: 2¼ hours
Oven: 150°C, 300°F, Gas Mark 2

Sauté the vegetables in 1 × 15 ml spoon (1 tablespoon) of
the oil, and place in the bottom of a casserole. Brown the
meat in the remaining oil and arrange over the vegetables.
Add the bouquet garni and season well. Mix the stock,
wine and Worcestershire sauce and pour over. Cover and
cook in oven for 2–2¼ hours. Taste and adjust the seasoning
and remove bouquet garni before serving.

Beef and lentil stew; Braised sliced beef; Beef cobbler

Beef cobbler

Metric	Imperial
4 × 15 ml spoons oil	4 tablespoons oil
450 g stewing steak, trimmed and cut into small cubes	1 lb stewing steak, trimmed and cut into small cubes
1 × 15 ml spoon seasoned flour	1 tablespoon seasoned flour
2 onions, peeled and diced	2 onions, peeled and diced
2 carrots, peeled and diced	2 carrots, peeled and diced
1 small turnip, peeled and diced	1 small turnip, peeled and diced
1 bay leaf	1 bay leaf
Salt and freshly ground black pepper	Salt and freshly ground black pepper
450 ml beef stock	$\frac{3}{4}$ pint beef stock

Scone topping:	Scone topping:
100 g flour	4 oz flour
$\frac{1}{4}$ teaspoon salt	$\frac{1}{4}$ teaspoon salt
50 g margarine	2 oz margarine
$\frac{1}{4}$ teaspoon mixed herbs	$\frac{1}{4}$ teaspoon mixed herbs
1 egg	1 egg
2 × 15 ml spoons milk	2 tablespoons milk

Cooking Time: $1\frac{1}{2}$ hours
Oven: 180°C, 350°F, Gas Mark 4
     220°C, 425°F, Gas Mark 7

Heat half the oil in a frying pan or casserole. Toss the meat in the flour and fry until golden brown on a fairly high heat. Turn down the heat, add remaining oil and vegetables, and sauté gently for a few minutes. Add the bay leaf, seasoning and stock and bring to the boil. Place in a casserole, if you have used a frying pan, cover and cook for 1 hour in the oven. Meanwhile sieve the flour and salt, then rub in the fat until the mixture resembles fine breadcrumbs. Add the herbs and mix with the egg and milk to a soft dough. Roll out on a floured board $2\frac{1}{2}$ cm (1 inch) thick and cut into rounds or triangles. Remove casserole from the oven, taste and adjust the seasoning. Turn up the heat and arrange scones on top. Return, uncovered, to the second top shelf of the oven for 15 minutes or until scone topping is golden brown.

Carbonnade of beef

Metric

700 g braising steak, trimmed and cut into 5 cm slices
1 × 15 ml spoon flour
Salt and freshly ground black pepper
50 g streaky bacon, rinded and diced
50 g butter
1 × 15 ml spoon oil
3 large onions, peeled and thinly sliced
300 ml brown ale
300 ml beef stock
1 × 5 ml spoon French mustard
Bouquet garni
Chopped parsley
8 slices French bread
4 × 5 ml spoons French mustard

Imperial

1½ lb braising steak, trimmed and cut into 2 inch slices
1 tablespoon flour
Salt and freshly ground black pepper
2 oz streaky bacon, rinded and diced
2 oz butter
1 tablespoon oil
3 large onions, peeled and thinly sliced
½ pint brown ale
½ pint beef stock
1 teaspoon French mustard
Bouquet garni
Chopped parsley
8 slices French bread
4 teaspoons French mustard

Cooking Time: 1¾–2 hours
Oven: 180°C, 350°F, Gas Mark 4

Toss steak in seasoned flour. Brown bacon in butter and oil and transfer to a casserole. Sauté onions in a frying pan then brown the beef on both sides, place in the casserole with the onions. Sprinkle remaining flour in the pan. Add ale, stock, and scrape juices from pan. Add to casserole with seasonings. Cook, covered, for 1½ hours or until tender in the oven. Remove bouquet garni. Taste and adjust seasoning, and consistency, if desired. Place French bread, spread with mustard, on the top. Cook, uncovered, for a further 15–20 minutes.

Carbonnade of beef

Red pepper and beef casserole

Metric	Imperial
450 g braising steak, trimmed and cut into 4 cm cubes	1 lb braising steak, trimmed and cut into 1½ inch cubes
2 × 15 ml spoons oil	2 tablespoons oil
25 g butter	1 oz butter
1 large onion, peeled and sliced	1 large onion, peeled and sliced
1 small carrot, peeled and sliced	1 small carrot, peeled and sliced
1 rasher bacon, rinded and diced	1 rasher bacon, rinded and diced
1 stick celery, washed and sliced	1 stick celery, washed and sliced
1 red pepper, washed and sliced	1 red pepper, washed and sliced
6 mushrooms, washed and sliced	6 mushrooms, washed and sliced
227 g can peeled tomatoes	8 oz can peeled tomatoes
4 bay leaves	4 bay leaves
¼ teaspoon dried marjoram	¼ teaspoon dried marjoram
Salt and freshly ground black pepper	Salt and freshly ground black pepper
300 ml boiling water	½ pint boiling water
1 beef stock cube	1 beef stock cube
4 × 15 ml spoons red wine	4 tablespoons red wine

Cooking Time: 1½–1¾ hours
Oven: 160°C, 325°F, Gas Mark 3

Fry the meat in hot oil, cooking quickly to ensure a good rich colour. Remove to a casserole. Add the butter to the pan and heat up. Sauté the onion, carrot, bacon and celery. Place over the meat, together with the pepper, mushrooms, tomatoes, herbs and seasoning. Make up the stock, add the red wine and pour over the casserole. Cover with a lid and cook for 1–1½ hours. Remove bay leaves. Taste and adjust seasoning before serving. Thicken with beurre manié if liked.

Red pepper and beef casserole

Tomato beef curry

Metric	Imperial
450 g braising steak, trimmed and cut into 2½ cm cubes	*1 lb braising steak, trimmed and cut into 1 inch cubes*
2 × 15 ml spoons oil	*2 tablespoons oil*
15 g butter	*½ oz butter*
1 large onion, peeled and sliced	*1 large onion, peeled and sliced*
1 carrot, peeled and sliced	*1 carrot, peeled and sliced*
2 × 15 ml spoons curry powder	*2 tablespoons curry powder*
1 × 15 ml spoon flour	*1 tablespoon flour*
1 × 15 ml spoon turmeric	*1 tablespoon turmeric*
396 g can tomatoes	*14 oz can tomatoes*
300–450 ml stock	*½–¾ pint stock*
Salt	*Salt*
4 bay leaves	*4 bay leaves*

Cooking Time: 1¾ hours
Oven: 160°C, 325°F, Gas Mark 3

Brown the meat in the oil over a brisk heat. Add the butter and sauté the onion and carrot until tender. Remove to a casserole with the meat. Add curry powder, flour, and turmeric and fry for 2 minutes. Stir in the tomatoes and stock. Cook and keep stirring from time to time until all juices are removed from the bottom of the pan. Season well with salt. Add to the casserole with the bay leaves. Cover and put in the oven to cook for 1½ hours. Remove bay leaves and taste and adjust seasoning before serving.

Madras meat and vegetable curry

Metric	Imperial
1 onion, peeled and diced	*1 onion, peeled and diced*
2 × 15 ml spoons oil	*2 tablespoons oil*
450 g chuck steak, trimmed and cubed	*1 lb chuck steak, trimmed and cubed*
1 × 15 ml spoon flour	*1 tablespoon flour*
1 clove garlic, crushed	*1 clove garlic, crushed*
1–2 × 15 ml spoons Madras curry powder	*1–2 tablespoons Madras curry powder*
¼ teaspoon chilli powder (optional)	*¼ teaspoon chilli powder (optional)*
300 ml stock	*½ pint stock*
1 × 5 ml spoon tomato purée	*1 teaspoon tomato purée*
1 potato, peeled and diced	*1 potato, peeled and diced*
½ teaspoon salt	*½ teaspoon salt*
4 cauliflower florets	*4 cauliflower florets*
To garnish:	**To garnish:**
1 small onion, peeled and sliced	*1 small onion, peeled and sliced*

Cooking Time: 1¾ hours
Oven: 160°C, 325°F, Gas Mark 3

Sauté the onion in oil, gently, and remove to a casserole. Toss the cubes of beef in flour and fry over a fairly high heat to brown. When brown lower the heat, add the crushed garlic and sprinkle with curry powder and chilli and allow to sauté for a few minutes. Pour on the stock mixed with tomato purée and transfer to the casserole when liquid begins to simmer. Add the potato, cover and simmer for 1 hour, add the salt. Add cauliflower and cover for the last 25–30 minutes of cooking. Taste and adjust seasoning before serving. Garnish with thinly sliced onion rings.
Accompaniments for curry are easy to obtain from the many Asian stores throughout the country.

Serve curries with:
Boiled or fried rice
Fried poppadums
Chapati – flat pancakes made from brown flour
Cucumber Raita – natural unsweetened yogurt with chopped cucumber
Sliced bananas, soaked in lemon juice
Mango chutney
Thinly sliced onion and tomato salad
Thinly sliced onion, tomato, and green pepper salad
Toasted coconut

Tomato beef curry; Madras meat and vegetable curry

Celery beef casserole with walnuts

Metric

450 g braising steak,
trimmed and cut into
2½ cm cubes
2 × 15 ml spoons oil
2 onions, peeled and diced
1 carrot, peeled and diced
15 g butter
1 × 15 ml spoon flour
300 ml stock
Salt and freshly ground
black pepper
1 head celery, washed and
sliced into 2½ cm lengths
½ teaspoon mixed herbs
1 × 15 ml spoon soured
cream

Imperial

1 lb braising steak,
trimmed and cut into
1 inch cubes
2 tablespoons oil
2 onions, peeled and diced
1 carrot, peeled and diced
½ oz butter
1 tablespoon flour
½ pint stock
Salt and freshly ground
black pepper
1 head celery, washed and
sliced into 1 inch lengths
½ teaspoon mixed herbs
1 tablespoon soured
cream

Cooking Time: 1½–2 hours
Oven: 150°C, 300°F, Gas Mark 2

Brown the meat in the oil and place in a casserole. Sauté the onions and carrots in the butter in the frying pan. Add the flour to make a roux and gradually add the stock, stirring with a wooden spoon until a smooth sauce is formed. Season well and pour over the meat. Add the celery and herbs. Cover and cook in the oven for 1½–1¾ hours. Just before serving taste and adjust the seasoning, add the soured cream and sprinkle with chopped walnuts.

Alabama chilli

Alabama chilli

Metric

1 × 15 ml spoon oil
450 g minced beef
2 onions, peeled and diced
1 carrot, peeled and diced
1 pepper, seeded and diced
1 chilli, seeded and diced
396 g can tomatoes
2–3 × 15 ml spoons
tomato purée
150 ml stock
1 bay leaf
½ teaspoon chilli powder
½ teaspoon mixed herbs
Salt and freshly ground
black pepper
250 g pkt frozen sweet
corn
396 g can kidney beans,
drained

Imperial

1 tablespoon oil
1 lb minced beef
2 onions, peeled and diced
1 carrot, peeled and diced
1 pepper, seeded and diced
1 chilli, seeded and diced
14 oz can tomatoes
2–3 tablespoons tomato
purée
¼ pint stock
1 bay leaf
½ teaspoon chilli powder
½ teaspoon mixed herbs
Salt and freshly ground
black pepper
8 oz pkt frozen sweet corn
14 oz can kidney beans,
drained

Cooking Time: 1 hour

Heat the oil in a frying pan and brown the meat. Transfer to a casserole. Sauté the onion, carrot, pepper and chilli and add to meat. Add remaining ingredients except for sweet-corn and kidney beans, season well. Cover and bring to the boil and simmer over a low heat for 45 minutes. Add the sweet corn and kidney beans and simmer for a further 15 minutes. Remove the bay leaf, taste and adjust the seasoning. Chilli powder may be adjusted to taste; a mild mixture will only require ¼ teaspoon. Serve with boiled rice or pasta.

16

Celery beef casserole with walnuts; Farmer's casserole

Farmer's casserole

Metric

2 × 15 ml spoons oil
450 g stewing steak,
trimmed and cut into
2½ cm cubes
2 carrots, peeled and diced
2 leeks, washed and sliced
1 onion, peeled and diced
15 g butter
300 ml stock
Salt and freshly ground
black pepper
396 g can butter
beans, drained
50 g frozen peas

For the cheese
dumplings:
100 g self raising flour
50 g suet, shredded
1 × 5 ml spoon finely
chopped parsley
50 g cheese, finely grated
Water to mix

Imperial

2 tablespoons oil
1 lb stewing steak,
trimmed and cut into
1 inch cubes
2 carrots, peeled and diced
2 leeks, washed and sliced
1 onion, peeled and diced
½ oz butter
½ pint stock
Salt and freshly ground
black pepper
14 oz can butter
beans, drained
2 oz frozen peas

For the cheese
dumplings:
4 oz self raising flour
2 oz suet, shredded
1 teaspoon finely
chopped parsley
2 oz cheese, finely grated
Water to mix

Cooking Time: 1½–2 hours
Oven: 180°C, 350°F, Gas Mark 4

Heat the oil in a frying pan and brown the meat. Transfer to a casserole. Sauté the vegetables in the butter in the frying pan and add to the meat. Stir in the stock and season well. Cover and cook in the oven for 1 hour. Meanwhile make the dumplings by putting all the dry ingredients in a bowl and mixing together with a little water to form a soft dough. Shape into 12 small dumplings. Remove the casserole from the oven. Stir in the butter beans and peas. Taste and adjust the seasoning. Arrange the dumplings over the top and put the uncovered casserole back in the oven for ½ hour or until the dumplings are golden brown.

Mexican beef

Metric

4 spring onions, washed
and chopped
4 × 15 ml spoons white
wine
2 × 15 ml spoons wine
vinegar
Salt and freshly ground
black pepper
1 × 5 ml spoon fresh
tarragon
4 American-style
beefburgers
1 × 15 ml spoon oil
½ teaspoon chilli
powder, to taste
25 g butter
1 onion, peeled and sliced
1 × 5 ml spoon flour
1 avocado pear, halved,
half diced and half thinly
sliced
2 × 15 ml spoons lemon
juice

Imperial

4 spring onions, washed
and chopped
4 tablespoons white wine
2 tablespoons wine vinegar
Salt and freshly ground
black pepper
1 teaspoon fresh tarragon
4 American-style
beefburgers
1 tablespoon oil
½ teaspoon chilli powder,
to taste
1 oz butter
1 onion, peeled and sliced
1 teaspoon flour
1 avocado pear, halved,
half diced and half thinly
sliced
2 tablespoons lemon juice

Cooking Time: 30 minutes

Make a marinade with the spring onions, wine, vinegar, seasoning and tarragon. Marinate the beefburgers for several hours. Remove and add to marinade the diced avocado. Heat the oil in a casserole, sprinkle with chilli powder and brown beefburgers quickly on each side. Add the butter and onion and sweat for a few minutes, sprinkle with flour and brown, pour in the strained marinade and cook, covered, for 15 minutes. Add the diced avocado and stir in gently. Taste and adjust the seasoning. Arrange the remaining slices of avocado on top of the meat, sprinkle with lemon juice and cook for a further 10 minutes.

Rough puff pastry

Metric

225 g strong plain flour
½ teaspoon salt
150 g margarine or butter
1 × 5 ml spoon lemon
juice
6–8 × 15 ml spoons water

Imperial

8 oz strong plain flour
½ teaspoon salt
6 oz margarine or butter
1 teaspoon lemon juice
6–8 tablespoons water

Cooking Time: 10–15 minutes.
Oven: 210°C, 425°F, Gas Mark 7

Sieve flour and salt together into a mixing bowl. Cut fat into small pieces, add to flour and toss lightly so each piece of fat is coated with flour. Add lemon juice and water to flour and fat and mix lightly with the blade of a knife making sure the pieces of fat are kept whole. If any loose flour remains, add a little more water and mix until the dough is soft. Gather the dough with the fingertips. Turn out onto a well floured board and sprinkle with flour.
Form into an oblong, flour the rolling pin and roll out to a strip about 38 cm (15 in) by 13 cm (5 in). Fold in 3 by folding the bottom third of the pastry upwards and the top third downwards and over the bottom fold.
Lightly press the three edges together with a rolling pin to seal.
Turn the pastry round so that the sealed right-hand edge faces you. Roll out to an oblong as before.
Brush off any surplus flour. Fold in three again and seal the edges. Sprinkle with flour, cover with a damp cloth and leave in a cool place for 20 minutes, until cool and firm.

Third and fourth rollings
Repeat as in second rolling a third and fourth time. After the last rolling and resting, the pastry is ready to roll out again to the required thickness and use.

Oranged steak and kidney casserole

Metric

2 × 15 ml spoons oil
1 onion, peeled and sliced
50 g mushrooms, washed
and sliced
450 g braising steak,
trimmed and cut into
2½ cm cubes
250 g kidney, cleaned,
cored and sliced
Finely grated rind of 1
orange
150 ml stock
Salt and freshly ground
black pepper
1 × 15 ml spoon
cornflour

To garnish:
1 × 15 ml spoon finely
chopped parsley
Squares of puff pastry
or rough puff pastry

Imperial

2 tablespoons oil
1 onion, peeled and sliced
2 oz mushrooms, washed
and sliced
1 lb braising steak,
trimmed and cut into
1 inch cubes
8 oz kidney, cleaned,
cored and sliced
Finely grated rind of 1
orange
¼ pint stock
Salt and freshly ground
black pepper
1 tablespoon cornflour

To garnish:
1 tablespoon finely
chopped parsley
Squares of puff pastry
or rough puff pastry

Cooking Time: 1¾ hours
Oven: 160°C, 325°F, Gas Mark 3

Heat the oil in a frying pan, sauté the onion and mushrooms in the oil for 3–4 minutes. Drain well and place in a casserole. Brown the steak and kidney over a fairly high heat to obtain good colour. Then place on top of vegetables. Add the grated orange rind, stock and seasoning to the frying pan and bring to the boil. Pour over the meat and vegetables. Cover the casserole and cook for 1½ hours. Blend the cornflour with a little water and thicken gravy, taste and adjust seasoning. Sprinkle with the parsley. Serve with squares of cooked puff or roughpuff pastry.

Mexican beef; Oranged steak and kidney casserole

Goulash

Metric	Imperial
2 × 15 ml spoons oil	2 tablespoons oil
450 g braising steak, trimmed and cubed	1 lb braising steak, trimmed and cubed
2 × 5 ml spoons paprika	2 teaspoons paprika
2 × 5 ml spoons flour	2 teaspoons flour
300 ml stock	½ pint stock
25 g butter	1 oz butter
225 g onions, peeled and diced	8 oz onions, peeled and diced
225 g carrots, scrubbed and diced	8 oz carrots, scrubbed and diced
1 bay leaf	1 bay leaf
Good pinch of thyme	Good pinch of thyme
396 g can tomatoes	14 oz can tomatoes
1 × 15 ml spoon tomato purée	1 tablespoon tomato purée
1 × 5 ml spoon lemon juice	1 teaspoon lemon juice
Salt and freshly ground black pepper	Salt and freshly ground black pepper
1 potato, peeled and diced	1 potato, peeled and diced
8 small onions, peeled	8 small onions, peeled
1 × 15 ml spoon soured cream	1 tablespoon soured cream
To garnish:	To garnish:
1 × 15 ml spoon finely chopped parsley	1 tablespoon finely chopped parsley

Cooking Time: 1¾–2 hours
Oven: 160°C, 325°F, Gas Mark 3

Heat the oil in a frying pan over a fairly high heat and fry the meat until brown on all sides. Reduce the heat, sprinkle with paprika and flour, turn the meat over to absorb the flour. After about 2–3 minutes pour the stock into the frying pan and stir gently. Pour into a casserole with the meat and meat particles. Rinse the pan, melt the butter and sweat the onions and carrots gently over a low heat. Add herbs, tomatoes, purée, lemon juice and seasoning. The potato can be made into balls or diced at this stage and added to the tomato mixture. Pour tomato mixture over the meat, cover casserole and cook in the oven for 1 hour. Remove casserole, add small onions and return for a further 45 minutes. Before serving remove bay leaf, taste and adjust the seasoning, stir in soured cream and sprinkle with parsley.

Herbed beef casserole

Metric	Imperial
2 × 15 ml spoons oil	2 tablespoons oil
1 large onion, peeled and sliced	1 large onion, peeled and sliced
1 large carrot, peeled and sliced	1 large carrot, peeled and sliced
450 g braising steak, trimmed and cut into 4 cm cubes	1 lb braising steak, trimmed and cut into 1½ inch cubes
25 g mushrooms, washed and sliced	1 oz mushrooms, washed and sliced
1 stick celery, washed and sliced	1 stick celery, washed and sliced
227 g can peeled tomatoes	8 oz can peeled tomatoes
1 × 15 ml spoon tomato purée	1 tablespoon tomato purée
1 × 5 ml spoon tarragon	1 teaspoon tarragon
1 × 5 ml spoon oregano	1 teaspoon oregano
1 bay leaf	1 bay leaf
Salt and freshly ground black pepper	Salt and freshly ground black pepper
300 ml boiling water	½ pint boiling water
1 beef stock cube	1 beef stock cube
Beurre manié	Beurre manié
25 g butter mixed with 2 × 15 ml spoons plain flour	1 oz butter mixed with 2 tablespoons plain flour

Cooking Time: 1¾ hours
Oven: 160°C, 325°F, Gas Mark 3

Preheat the oven. Heat the oil in a frying pan and fry the onion and carrot until the onion is soft. Remove the vegetables and place in a casserole. Brown the meat quickly in the hot fat to seal in the juices, then add to the vegetables, together with mushrooms and celery. Add tomatoes, tomato purée and herbs. Season with salt and pepper. Make up the stock and pour over the contents of the casserole. Cover with the lid and place in the oven for 1½ hours. Taste and adjust seasoning and thicken with a beurre manié before serving.

Herbed beef casserole; Goulash

Fluffy mince casserole

Metric	Imperial
1 × 15 ml spoon oil	1 tablespoon oil
25 g butter	1 oz butter
2 onions, peeled and diced	2 onions, peeled and diced
50 g mushrooms, washed and chopped (optional)	2 oz mushrooms, washed and chopped (optional)
450 g lean minced beef	1 lb lean minced beef
1 × 15 ml spoon flour	1 tablespoon flour
150 ml stock	¼ pint stock
½ teaspoon mixed herbs (optional)	½ teaspoon mixed herbs (optional)
2 × 5 ml spoons Worcestershire sauce	2 teaspoons Worcestershire sauce
Salt and freshly ground black pepper	Salt and freshly ground black pepper
350 g cooked, mashed potatoes	12 oz cooked, mashed potatoes
2 eggs, separated	2 eggs, separated
25 g cheese, grated	1 oz cheese, grated

Cooking Time: 1 hour
Oven: 190°C, 375°F, Gas Mark 5

Heat the oil and butter in a frying pan and sauté the onions and mushrooms for about 4 minutes. Remove to a casserole, brown the minced beef, sprinkle with flour, add the stock, Worcestershire sauce and seasoning and simmer for a few minutes, then pour into the casserole. Beat the potatoes with seasoning and egg yolks until creamy and free from lumps. Whisk the egg whites until light and fluffy and fold into the potatoes. Fork on to the meat mixture and cook, uncovered, on the middle shelf of the oven, sprinkled with grated cheese for 45 minutes.

Fluffy mince casserole; Highland casserole

Highland casserole

Metric	Imperial
2 × 15 ml spoons oil	2 tablespoons oil
450 g braising steak, trimmed and cut into 2½ cm cubes	1 lb braising steak, trimmed and cut into 1 inch cubes
2 onions, peeled and diced	2 onions, peeled and diced
1 carrot, peeled and diced	1 carrot, peeled and diced
1 turnip, peeled and diced	1 turnip, peeled and diced
50 g pearl barley	2 oz pearl barley
1 × 15 ml spoon Worcestershire sauce	1 tablespoon Worcestershire sauce
450 ml stock	¾ pint stock
2 bay leaves	2 bay leaves
Salt and freshly ground black pepper	Salt and freshly ground black pepper
To garnish:	To garnish:
Parsley	Parsley

Cooking Time: 1½–1¾ hours
Oven: 180°C, 350°F, Gas Mark 4

Heat the oil in a frying pan and brown the meat. Lower heat add the vegetables and cook for about 3 minutes. Transfer to a casserole and add the remaining ingredients. Cover and cook for 1½ hours. Taste and adjust the seasoning, remove bay leaves, and serve garnished with parsley.

Beef provençale

Beef provençale

Metric	Imperial
2 × 15 ml spoons oil	2 tablespoons oil
450 g braising steak, trimmed and cut into 2½ cm cubes	1 lb braising steak, trimmed and cut into 1 inch cubes
1½ onions, peeled and sliced	1½ onions, peeled and sliced
¼ red or green pepper, seeded and diced	¼ red or green pepper, seeded and diced
1 large tomato, washed and sliced	1 large tomato, washed and sliced
1 large carrot, scraped and diced	1 large carrot, scraped and diced
4 small mushrooms	4 small mushrooms
1 slice streaky bacon, rinded and diced	1 slice streaky bacon, rinded and diced
25 g butter	1 oz butter

Stock:

Metric	Imperial
300 ml water	½ pint water
4 × 15 ml spoons red wine	4 tablespoons red wine
1 × 5 ml spoon tomato purée	1 teaspoon tomato purée
2 × 5 ml spoons salt	2 teaspoons salt
1 × 5 ml spoon oregano	1 teaspoon oregano
1 × 5 ml spoon thyme	1 teaspoon thyme
Freshly ground black pepper	Freshly ground black pepper

Cooking Time: 1¾–2 hours
Oven: 160°C, 325°F, Gas Mark 3

Heat the oil in a frying pan and fry meat until browned and sealed. Transfer to a casserole dish. Fry all the diced and sliced vegetables gently in the butter in the frying pan, at the same time adding the diced bacon. When the vegetables are soft, add contents of frying pan to the casserole. Make up the stock by placing all the ingredients in a saucepan and bringing to the boil. Add to the casserole. Cover and cook in the oven for 1½–1¾ hours. Taste and adjust the seasoning, thicken with beurre manié if necessary before serving.

23

Italian beef casserole

Metric	Imperial
1 medium-sized onion, peeled and sliced	1 medium-sized onion, peeled and sliced
1 large carrot, scraped and diced	1 large carrot, scraped and diced
2 × 15 ml spoons oil	2 tablespoons oil
450 g braising steak, trimmed and cut into 2½ cm cubes	1 lb braising steak, trimmed and cut into 1 inch cubes
25 g mushrooms, washed and sliced	1 oz mushrooms, washed and sliced
175 g can tomatoes	7 oz can tomatoes
¼ red pepper, seeded and sliced	¼ red pepper, seeded and sliced
300 ml boiling water	½ pint boiling water
1 beef stock cube	1 beef stock cube
1 × 15 ml spoon tomato purée	1 tablespoon tomato purée
½ teaspoon oregano	½ teaspoon oregano
1 bay leaf	1 bay leaf
Salt and freshly ground black pepper	Salt and freshly ground black pepper
1 × 15 ml spoon flour	1 tablespoon flour
15 g butter	½ oz butter

Cooking Time: 1½ hours
Oven: 160°C, 325°F, Gas Mark 3

Sauté vegetables in the oil until tender. Drain and place in the bottom of a casserole. Fry the meat until brown to seal in the juices. Place on top of the vegetables. Lay the mushrooms on top of the meat. Add the tomatoes to the casserole. Place the sliced peppers over the mushrooms. Make up the stock, add tomato purée and pour in. Add the herbs and bay leaf, season well and stir to mix. Cover and put into the oven. Remove after 1 hour and taste and adjust the seasoning. Thicken with a beurre manié, make sure gravy is smooth and free from lumps and continue cooking for a further 15–20 minutes or until meat is tender. Remove the bay leaf before serving.

Burgundian beef

Metric	Imperial
450 g top rump beef, trimmed and cut into 2½ cm cubes	1 lb top rump beef, trimmed and cut into 1 inch cubes
2 onions, peeled and thinly sliced	2 onions, peeled and thinly sliced
2 carrots, peeled and thinly sliced	2 carrots, peeled and thinly sliced
6 peppercorns	6 peppercorns
3 parsley sprigs	3 parsley sprigs
¼ teaspoon dried thyme	¼ teaspoon dried thyme
1 bay leaf	1 bay leaf
300 ml Burgundy	½ pint Burgundy
2 × 15 ml spoons oil	2 tablespoons oil
25 g butter	1 oz butter
16 small button onions	16 small button onions
2 slices streaky bacon, rinded and cut into strips	2 slices streaky bacon, rinded and cut into strips
2 × 15 ml spoons brandy	2 tablespoons brandy
2 × 15 ml spoons flour	2 tablespoons flour
1 clove garlic, crushed	1 clove garlic, crushed
150 ml stock	¼ pint stock
Salt and freshly ground black pepper	Salt and freshly ground black pepper
Bouquet garni	Bouquet garni
100 g mushrooms, washed and sliced	4 oz mushrooms, washed and sliced

To garnish:
2 × 15 ml spoons finely chopped parsley

To garnish:
2 tablespoons finely chopped parsley

Cooking Time: 1¼–1½ hours
Oven: 160°C, 325°F, Gas Mark 3

Marinate the meat in a bowl with the onions, carrots, peppercorns, herbs and half the wine for about 12 hours. Turn over from time to time. Heat the oil and butter in a frying pan and fry the onions and bacon strips until golden brown, remove to a casserole. Drain the meat from the marinade and brown over a fairly high heat in the frying pan. Ignite brandy and pour over the meat. Sprinkle the meat with flour, add the crushed garlic then pour over the marinade, remaining wine and stock. When the liquid is simmering pour into the casserole. Add seasoning, bouquet garni and mushrooms. Cover and simmer for 1–1¼ hours. Taste and adjust seasoning. Put meat on a serving dish with onions and mushrooms. Remove the bay leaf and bouquet garni. Reduce the gravy slightly and strain over the meat. Sprinkle with chopped parsley.

Italian beef casserole; Burgundian beef

New England boiled dinner

Metric

2 × 15 ml spoons oil
2 onions, peeled and sliced
2 carrots, peeled and sliced
1 turnip, peeled and sliced
1 leek, washed and sliced
1½ kg rolled silverside of beef
Bouquet garni
600 ml beef stock
Salt and freshly ground black pepper
8 medium-sized potatoes, peeled
8 small carrots, peeled
1 small white cabbage, washed and cut into 8 wedges

Imperial

2 tablespoons oil
2 onions, peeled and sliced
2 carrots, peeled and sliced
1 turnip, peeled and sliced
1 leek, washed and sliced
3½ lb rolled silverside of beef
Bouquet garni
1 pint beef stock
Salt and freshly ground black pepper
8 medium-sized potatoes, peeled
8 small carrots, peeled
1 small white cabbage, washed and cut into 8 wedges

Cooking Time: 1½–2 hours
Oven: 160°C, 325°F, Gas Mark 3

Heat the oil in a large casserole and sauté the sliced vegetables, push to the side and brown the meat on all sides. Add bouquet garni, stock and seasoning. Cover and cook for 30 minutes. Add potatoes and carrots, baste well with the liquid, cover and cook for a further 40 minutes. Lastly add the cabbage and cook for a further 15 minutes. Taste and adjust seasoning, remove bouquet garni. Serve on a heated dish surrounded by whole vegetables. The casseroled vegetables may be served with the meat also. Serves 6.

Yorkshire Topside casserole

Metric

2 × 15 ml spoons oil
2 onions, peeled and diced
1 carrot, washed and sliced
1 leek, washed and sliced
3 sticks celery, washed and sliced
1½ kg topside of beef
600 ml beef stock
Bouquet garni
Salt and freshly ground black pepper
1 × 5 ml spoon Worcestershire sauce

Imperial

2 tablespoons oil
2 onions, peeled and diced
1 carrot, washed and sliced
1 leek, washed and sliced
3 sticks celery, washed and sliced
3½ lb topside of beef
1 pint beef stock
Bouquet garni
Salt and freshly ground black pepper
1 teaspoon Worcestershire sauce

Cooking Time: 1½ hours
Oven: 190°C, 375°F, Gas Mark 5
220°C, 425°F, Gas Mark 7

Heat the oil and sauté the sliced vegetables in a large casserole, push to the side and brown the meat on all sides, pour in the stock, herbs and seasonings. Cook, covered for 1 hour. Taste and adjust seasoning. Remove bouquet garni. Serve the sliced beef, vegetables from the casserole, gravy and horseradish sauce with Yorkshire pudding.
This is an ideal way to cook lean topside, which tends to be dry when roasted. Serves 6.

New England boiled dinner; Yorkshire puddings; Yorkshire topside casserole

Yorkshire pudding

Metric

125 g flour
½ teaspoon salt
2 eggs
300 ml milk
25 g cooking fat

Imperial

4 oz flour
½ teaspoon salt
2 eggs
½ pint milk
1 oz cooking fat

Cooking Time: small 15 minutes, large 30–45 minutes.
Oven: 210°C, 425°F, Gas Mark 7

Make up the batter by sieving the flour and salt into a bowl. Make a well in the centre of the flour, drop in the beaten egg and half the milk. Mix thoroughly, beating so that all the flour is absorbed gradually and until mixture is thick, smooth and creamy. Lightly beat in the remaining milk and use as required.

For small puddings heat the fat in the patty tins until it is very hot, then pour in the batter. Bake on the second top shelf of the oven until well risen and golden brown.

27

Bolognese sauce

Metric	Imperial
2 × 15 ml spoons oil	2 tablespoons oil
1 rasher streaky bacon, rinded and cut finely	1 rasher streaky bacon, rinded and cut finely
2 onions, peeled and finely diced	2 onions, peeled and finely diced
1 clove garlic, crushed	1 clove garlic, crushed
1 small carrot, peeled and diced	1 small carrot, peeled and diced
1 stick celery, washed and thinly sliced	1 stick celery, washed and thinly sliced
450 g minced beef	1 lb minced beef
50 g chicken livers, finely chopped	2 oz chicken livers, finely chopped
396 g can tomatoes	14 oz can tomatoes
2 × 15 ml spoons tomato purée	2 tablespoons tomato purée
1 bay leaf	1 bay leaf
1 × 5 ml spoon oregano	1 teaspoon oregano
2 × 15 ml spoons red wine	2 tablespoons red wine
150 ml chicken stock	¼ pint chicken stock
Salt and freshly ground black pepper	Salt and freshly ground black pepper

Cooking Time: 1–1¼ hours
Oven: 180°C, 350°F, Gas Mark 4

Heat the oil in a frying pan. Fry the bacon until golden. Add onions, garlic, carrot, and celery and allow to cook gently for 4 minutes, then remove to a casserole. Brown the beef on a brisk heat, then add the chicken livers and allow to brown, add tomatoes, allow to heat through and pour into a casserole. Mix the purée, herbs and wine with the stock, pour into the frying pan to heat and remove any meat juice which was left behind. Season well, pour over meat, cover and simmer for 45 minutes on top of cooker or 1 hour in the oven. Taste and adjust seasoning. Remove bay leaf. Serve with 225–350 g (8–12 oz) of cooked spaghetti which has been boiled in plenty of salted boiling water for 12 minutes. Drain well then toss in a little butter, with a little freshly ground pepper and a little nutmeg. Serve with grated cheese.

Use the automatic oven for Bolognese sauce to save time in the evenings.

Béchamel sauce

Metric	Imperial
600 ml milk	1 pint milk
1 small carrot, peeled and sliced	1 small carrot, peeled and sliced
1 onion, peeled, quartered and stuck with 4 cloves	1 onion, peeled, quartered and stuck with 4 cloves
6 peppercorns	6 peppercorns
1 bay leaf	1 bay leaf
50 g butter	2 oz butter
50 g flour	2 oz flour
Salt and freshly ground black pepper	Salt and freshly ground black pepper

Cooking Time: 35 minutes

Place the milk in a saucepan with the carrot, onion, peppercorns and bay leaf. Heat the milk on a very low heat until just under boiling, simmer for a few minutes then cover and allow to stand for 15–30 minutes. Strain the milk; melt the butter in a clean saucepan, add the flour and beat well until a roux is formed, gradually whisk or beat in the milk over a low heat until a smooth sauce is obtained, taste and adjust the seasoning.

Cannelloni

Metric	Imperial
8 tubes of non-boil cannelloni, 15 cm long	8 tubes of non-boil cannelloni, 6 inches long
½ quantity Bolognese sauce	½ quantity Bolognese sauce
1 × 5 ml spoon oil	1 teaspoon oil
600 ml Béchamel sauce	1 pint Béchamel sauce
Salt and freshly ground black pepper	Salt and freshly ground black pepper
2 × 15 ml spoons single cream	2 tablespoons single cream
50 g cheese, grated	2 oz cheese, grated

Cooking Time: 1¾ hours
Oven: 180°C, 350°F, Gas Mark 4

Stuff the tubes of cannelloni with Bolognese sauce and arrange in an oiled casserole dish. Pour on the Béchamel sauce and season well. Cover and cook in the oven for 30 minutes. Sprinkle with cream and grated cheese and return to the oven, uncovered, for 15 minutes. Place under the grill to brown the top, if preferred.

Variation

Some people may prefer the more traditional Italian cannelloni stuffed with spinach and ricotta cheese and topped with a Béchamel sauce.

Cannelloni with Béchamel sauce; Spaghetti with Bolognese sauce

Lamb is available to us all the year round, either home produced or from New Zealand. It makes delicious casseroles as long, slow cooking is ideal for the less tender cuts. However lamb tends to have lots of fat so it is best to skim after cooking.
Suitable cuts for the casserole: Shoulder, Scrag end, Middle neck, Leg, Shank end and Breast.

Australian fruit casserole

Metric

8 small lamb chops
15 g butter
1 clove garlic, crushed
1 small onion, peeled and diced
1 × 15 ml spoon honey
½ teaspoon dry mustard
1 small apple, diced
1 small piece root ginger, chopped
50 g raisins
150 ml chicken stock
1 × 5 ml spoon cornflour
Salt and freshly ground black pepper

To garnish:

1 red apple, sliced
1 × 15 ml spoon lemon juice

Imperial

8 small lamb chops
½ oz butter
1 clove garlic, crushed
1 small onion, peeled and diced
1 tablespoon honey
½ teaspoon dry mustard
1 small apple, diced
1 small piece root ginger, chopped
2 oz raisins
¼ pint chicken stock
1 teaspoon cornflour
Salt and freshly ground black pepper

To garnish:

1 red apple, sliced
1 tablespoon lemon juice

Cooking Time: 40 minutes
Oven: 180°C, 350°F, Gas Mark 4

Grill the chops under a preheated high grill for 2 minutes each side to brown and remove fat. Heat the butter in a casserole, add garlic and onion and cook for 3–4 minutes on a low heat. Add the honey and mustard, remove from the heat and coat chops in the honey and onion mixture. Arrange in the casserole, add apple, ginger and raisins. Mix stock with cornflour, season well, bring to the boil and pour over the chops. Cover and cook in the oven for 30 minutes, taste and adjust the seasoning. Garnish with a sliced red apple which has been dipped in lemon juice.

Braised chops in mint jelly

Metric

8 loin chops, boned and rolled
1 large onion, peeled and sliced
Few mint leaves
Salt and freshly ground black pepper
300 ml stock or water

Jelly:

300 ml stock from the chops
A good bunch of fresh mint leaves, washed and chopped
5 × 15 ml spoons wine vinegar
5 × 5 ml spoons gelatine
4 × 15 ml spoons very hot water

Imperial

8 loin chops, boned and rolled
1 large onion, peeled and sliced
Few mint leaves
Salt and freshly ground black pepper
½ pint stock or water

Jelly:

½ pint stock from the chops
A good bunch of fresh mint leaves, washed and chopped
5 tablespoons wine vinegar
5 teaspoons gelatine
4 tablespoons very hot water

Cooking Time: 50 minutes
Oven: 160°C, 325°F, Gas Mark 3

Fry the chops in a casserole to brown on each side, without fat. Add the onion, the mint leaves, seasoning and stock. Bring to the boil, cover and cook in the oven for 40 minutes. Remove the chops, cool and place on a serving dish in the refrigerator. Cool the stock from the chops and skim away the fat. Add the mint and wine vinegar. Dissolve the gelatine thoroughly by sprinkling in hot water, add to the mint liquid and pour over rolled chops. Allow to set and serve with salad and new potatoes.

Australian fruit casserole; Braised chops in mint jelly

Braised loin of lamb

Metric

Salt and freshly ground black pepper
1 loin of lamb, boned, rolled and tied
1 × 15 ml spoon oil
25 g butter
225 g haricot beans, soaked
2 large carrots, peeled and diced
1 turnip, peeled and diced
1 bay leaf
300 ml stock
25 g butter
25 g flour

To garnish:
4 tomatoes, skinned
Parsley

Imperial

Salt and freshly ground black pepper
1 loin of lamb, boned, rolled and tied
1 tablespoon oil
1 oz butter
8 oz haricot beans, soaked
2 large carrots, peeled and diced
1 turnip, peeled and diced
1 bay leaf
½ pint stock
1 oz butter
1 oz flour

To garnish:
4 tomatoes, skinned
Parsley

Cooking Time: 1¾ hours
Oven: 180°C, 350°F, Gas Mark 4

Season meat well with salt and pepper. Brown meat on all sides in the melted oil and butter in a casserole. Remove meat. Fry vegetables quickly in hot fat. Replace meat on top of vegetables in casserole, add bay leaf and stock and cover the pan. Cook gently in the oven for 1½ hours. Taste and adjust the seasoning. Remove the bay leaf. Remove meat, serve on dish surrounded by strained vegetables. Garnish with tomatoes and parsley. Make a sauce with butter, flour, and strained vegetable stock. Taste and adjust seasoning and serve in a heated sauce boat.

Indian lamb

Metric

700 g shoulder of lamb, boned and cut into 2½ cm cubes
½ teaspoon ground coriander
½ teaspoon cardamom
½ teaspoon poppy seeds
½ teaspoon ground cinnamon
¼ teaspoon ground cloves
½ teaspoon salt
½ teaspoon ground black pepper
5 cm piece stem ginger, finely chopped
2 cloves garlic, crushed
300 ml natural yogurt
15 g butter
1 large onion, peeled and finely chopped
25 g flaked almonds

To garnish:
Chopped parsley
1 small onion, peeled, sliced into rings

Imperial

1½ lb shoulder of lamb, boned and cut into 1 inch cubes
½ teaspoon ground coriander
½ teaspoon cardamom
½ teaspoon poppy seeds
½ teaspoon ground cinnamon
¼ teaspoon ground cloves
½ teaspoon salt
½ teaspoon ground black pepper
2 inch piece stem ginger, finely chopped
2 cloves garlic, crushed
½ pint natural yogurt
½ oz butter
1 large onion, peeled and finely chopped
1 oz flaked almonds

To garnish:
Chopped parsley
1 small onion, peeled and sliced into rings

Cooking Time: 1¼ hours
Oven: 160°C, 325°F, Gas Mark 3

Place the lamb in a bowl with the coriander, cardamon, poppy seeds, cinnamon, cloves, salt and pepper, ginger and garlic. Mix well then add the yogurt. Leave lamb to marinate in this mixture for several hours, in a casserole. Heat the butter, fry the chopped onion until just beginning to brown, do not burn, add the almonds. Transfer to a plate. Remove meat from the marinade and brown, return to casserole. Add the remaining marinade to the frying pan, stir well and pour over the meat in the casserole. Rinse out frying pan with a little water to obtain all juices, add to the casserole with fried onion rings and almonds. Cover and simmer for 1 hour or until the meat is tender. Serve on a bed of saffron rice garnished with parsley and onion rings.

Braised loin of lamb; Indian lamb; Casseroled loin chops

Casseroled loin chops

Metric

2 onions, peeled and sliced
2 × 5 ml spoons oil
¼ teaspoon cinnamon
¼ teaspoon cloves
1 clove garlic, crushed
225 g tomatoes, skinned
and sliced
Salt and freshly ground
black pepper
4 lamb chops

Imperial

2 onions, peeled and sliced
2 teaspoons oil
¼ teaspoon cinnamon
¼ teaspoon cloves
1 clove garlic, crushed
8 oz tomatoes, skinned
and sliced
Salt and freshly ground
black pepper
4 lamb chops

Cooking Time: 1 hour
Oven: 160°C, 325°F, Gas Mark 3

Fry the onions in the oil in a frying pan until golden brown.
Add the spices, garlic, tomatoes and seasoning. Cook for a
few minutes, add the chops. Transfer to a casserole, cover
and cook in the oven for ¾–1 hour.

Lamb and aubergine casserole

Metric

4 medium-sized
aubergines, washed
1 × 15 ml spoon oil
450 g minced lamb
1 large onion, peeled and
finely diced
1 clove garlic, crushed
(optional)
2 × 15 ml spoons parsley,
finely chopped
½ teaspoon dried rosemary
Salt and freshly ground
black pepper
2 × 396 g cans tomatoes,
sieved or liquidised
½ teaspoon Worcestershire
sauce

Imperial

4 medium-sized
aubergines, washed
1 tablespoon oil
1 lb minced lamb
1 large onion, peeled and
finely diced
1 clove garlic, crushed
(optional)
2 tablespoons parsley,
finely chopped
½ teaspoon dried rosemary
Salt and freshly ground
black pepper
2 × 14 oz cans tomatoes,
sieved or liquidised
½ teaspoon Worcestershire
sauce

Cooking Time: 40 minutes
Oven: 180°C, 350°F, Gas Mark 4

Cut the aubergines in half lengthwise and scoop out the central core leaving a fairly thick shell. Blanch the halves for 1 minute in boiling water, then arrange in a casserole. Dice the remaining flesh. Heat the oil in a frying pan, add the minced lamb and brown lightly over a brisk heat. Add the aubergine, onion and garlic and turn down the heat, mix well turning over until the onion becomes opaque. Add the parsley, rosemary and seasoning, mix well and remove from heat. Fill aubergine halves with lamb mixture. Sieve or liquidise the tomatoes, season well, add Worcestershire sauce and pour over aubergines. Cover the casserole and cook. Taste and adjust seasoning.

Tarragon lamb; Irish stew

Lamb and aubergine casserole

Irish stew

Metric

2 large onions, peeled and sliced
1 kg scrag end of neck of lamb, cut into slices
2 × 5 ml spoons mixed dried herbs (optional)
Salt and freshly ground black pepper
2–3 large potatoes, peeled and sliced
600 ml stock or water

To garnish:
1 × 15 ml spoon finely chopped parsley

Imperial

2 large onions, peeled and sliced
2 lb scrag end of neck of lamb, cut into slices
2 teaspoons mixed dried herbs (optional)
Salt and freshly ground black pepper
2–3 large potatoes, peeled and sliced
1 pint stock or water

To garnish:
1 tablespoon finely chopped parsley

Cooking Time: 1½ hours
Oven: 180°C, 350°F, Gas Mark 4

Place some sliced onion in a casserole, with the lamb on top. Sprinkle with herbs, if desired, season well. Add remaining onions and sliced potatoes mixed, season well, pour in stock. Place in the oven, covered, for 1¼ hours. Uncover for remaining 15 minutes, to allow the top to brown slightly. Serve sprinkled with freshly chopped parsley and colourful vegetables such as peas and carrots. It is most important that this dish is seasoned well.

Tarragon lamb

Metric

65 g butter
1 kg leg of lamb
450 ml veal or white stock
150 ml dry white wine
1 bouquet fresh tarragon
Salt and freshly ground black pepper
1½ × 15 ml spoons cornflour
2 × 15 ml spoons of cream (optional)

Imperial

2½ oz butter
2 lb leg of lamb
¾ pint veal or white stock
¼ pint dry white wine
1 bouquet fresh tarragon
Salt and freshly ground black pepper
1½ tablespoons cornflour
2 tablespoons of cream (optional)

Cooking Time: 1–1¼ hours
Oven: 180°C, 350°F, Gas Mark 4

Heat 40 g (1½ oz) of the butter in a casserole and seal the leg of lamb on all sides. Add the remainder of the butter, the stock and wine. Cover and cook for ¾ hour. Remove the meat and reduce the liquid by half. Add the tarragon and seasoning. Thicken with the cornflour and add the cream, if used. Taste and adjust the seasoning, remove the tarragon. Slice the lamb and serve with sauce poured over.

Lamb with dill sauce

Metric	Imperial
700 g leg or shoulder of lamb cut into 2½ cm cubes	1½ lb leg or shoulder of lamb cut into 1 inch cubes
2 × 5 ml spoons salt	2 teaspoons salt
5–6 peppercorns	5–6 peppercorns
Bunch of dill	Bunch of dill
2 carrots, peeled and thinly sliced	2 carrots, peeled and thinly sliced
2 onions, peeled and thinly sliced	2 onions, peeled and thinly sliced
2 parsnips, peeled and thinly sliced	2 parsnips, peeled and thinly sliced
50 g butter	2 oz butter
50 g flour	2 oz flour
600 ml reserved stock	1 pint reserved stock
2 × 15 ml spoons white vinegar	2 tablespoons white vinegar
1 × 15 ml spoon sugar	1 tablespoon sugar
Salt and freshly ground black pepper	Salt and freshly ground black pepper
1 egg yolk	1 egg yolk
3 × 15 ml spoons double cream	3 tablespoons double cream

Cooking Time: 1¼ hours approx.
Oven: 160°C, 325°F, Gas Mark 3

Place the meat in a large casserole, cover with water, bring to the boil. Remove any scum. Add salt, peppercorns and the dill stalks. Cover and cook over a slow heat until tender or in the oven. Add the carrots, onions and parsnips and continue cooking for 20–30 minutes until vegetables are just cooked. Drain the meat and vegetables and reserve the stock. Keep the meat and vegetables warm. Melt the butter in a saucepan. Add the flour. Cook for a few minutes but do not brown. Add the pint of meat stock, stirring constantly until the sauce is smooth and thick. Add the vinegar and sugar and season to taste. Mix the egg yolk with the cream in a small bowl. Add this to the sauce beating constantly simmer gently for 4–5 minutes, but do not boil. Add the meat and 2–3 tablespoons finely chopped dill. Taste and adjust the seasoning. Serve with the chopped vegetables.

Creamed lamb with cucumber

Metric	Imperial
1 kg lean cooked lamb, diced	2 lb lean cooked lamb, diced
3 spring onions or 1 small onion, finely sliced	3 spring onions or 1 small onion, finely sliced
1½ × 5 ml spoons salt	1½ teaspoons salt
Freshly ground black pepper	Freshly ground black pepper
1 egg, hard-boiled	1 egg, hard-boiled
1 cucumber, washed	1 cucumber, washed
¼ teaspoon nutmeg	¼ teaspoon nutmeg
¼ teaspoon basil	¼ teaspoon basil
Good pinch dill	Good pinch dill
Mint	Mint
25 g butter	1 oz butter
2 × 15 ml spoons cider vinegar	2 tablespoons cider vinegar
50 g butter	2 oz butter
50 g flour	2 oz flour
600 ml milk	1 pint milk
1 × 5 ml spoon lemon juice	1 teaspoon lemon juice

To garnish:
Bacon rashers, rinded

To garnish:
Bacon rashers, rinded

Cooking Time: 50 minutes
Oven: 180°C, 350°F, Gas Mark 4

Combine lamb and onions, season well. Hard boil the egg. Cut the cucumber in half lengthwise. Remove the seeds cut into 1 inch slices. Season with nutmeg, basil, dill and a little chopped mint. Heat the butter in a casserole. Add cucumber, salt and vinegar, cover and simmer gently for 10 minutes. Remove cover and slightly increase heat to a rapid boil to reduce the liquid a little. The cucumber should then be tender, but not brown. Reduce heat, stir in the lamb, heat gently in the oven for 20 minutes. Prepare sauce by making a roux with the butter and flour, then adding milk and stirring over a low heat until the mixture thickens. Add chopped egg and lemon juice to the sauce. Combine the lamb and cucumber with the sauce and simmer gently for 20 minutes. Taste and adjust the seasoning. Serve garnished with grilled bacon rolls and sautéed potatoes.

Creamed lamb with cucumber; Lamb with dill sauce; Lamb chops rosemary

Lamb chops rosemary

Metric

1 × 15 ml spoon French mustard
1 × 5 ml spoon soy sauce
½ teaspoon chopped fresh rosemary or ¼ teaspoon dried
¼ teaspoon dried ginger
1 clove garlic, crushed
Salt and freshly ground black pepper
2 × 15 ml spoons white wine
2 × 15 ml spoons cider vinegar
4 chump or leg chops
2 × 15 ml spoons water
1 × 5 ml spoon cornflour
2 × 15 ml spoons single cream
½ teaspoon brown sugar

To garnish:
Rosemary sprigs

Imperial

1 tablespoon French mustard
1 teaspoon soy sauce
½ teaspoon chopped fresh rosemary or ¼ teaspoon dried
¼ teaspoon dried ginger
1 clove garlic, crushed
Salt and freshly ground black pepper
2 tablespoons white wine
2 tablespoons cider vinegar
4 chump or leg chops
2 tablespoons water
1 teaspoon cornflour
2 tablespoons single cream
½ teaspoon brown sugar

To garnish:
Rosemary sprigs

Cooking Time: 40 minutes
Oven: 160°C, 325°F, Gas Mark 3

Mix the mustard, soy sauce, rosemary, ginger, garlic, seasoning, wine and vinegar together. Spread on the chops and allow to marinate for several hours. Brown chops on both sides without oil. Pour over marinade and water. Cook in the oven, covered, for 35 minutes. Taste and adjust seasoning. Thicken liquid with cornflour. Pour on cream and sprinkle with brown sugar. Return to the oven for 5 minutes and serve garnished with sprigs of rosemary. Delicious with baked potatoes and peas.

37

Greek shepherd's pie

Metric

1 large aubergine, washed
and sliced
1 × 15 ml spoon lemon
juice
50 g butter
2 onions, peeled and
thinly sliced
1 large potato, peeled and
thinly sliced
450 g minced lamb
2 tomatoes, peeled and
sliced
300 ml Béchamel sauce
(page 29)
Salt and freshly ground
black pepper
50 g cheese, grated

Imperial

1 large aubergine, washed
and sliced
1 tablespoon lemon juice
2 oz butter
2 onions, peeled and
thinly sliced
1 large potato, peeled and
thinly sliced
1 lb minced lamb
2 tomatoes, peeled and
sliced
½ pint Béchamel sauce
(page 29)
Salt and freshly ground
black pepper
2 oz cheese, grated

Cooking Time: 1 hour
Oven: 160°C, 325°F, Gas Mark 3

Arrange the sliced aubergine on a plate, sprinkle with a little salt and lemon juice and allow to stand for 15 minutes. Heat the butter and gently fry the onions first then the aubergines and finally the potato, without breaking the slices, for a few minutes. Remove each batch to a plate as fried. Brown the lamb. Place a layer of aubergine and onion in a casserole, then lamb and tomatoes, a little sauce, and season well. Then layer potatoes, lamb and a little sauce. Finish with aubergines, tomatoes and remaining sauce, sprinkle with grated cheese and cook, uncovered, for 45 minutes.

Leek and lamb casserole; Greek shepherd's pie

Lamb with pineapple

Lamb with pineapple

Metric	Imperial
25 g butter	1 oz butter
2 small onions, peeled and diced	2 small onions, peeled and diced
1 × 15 ml spoon mild curry powder	1 tablespoon mild curry powder
1 × 15 ml spoon flour	1 tablespoon flour
300 ml stock or water	½ pint stock or water
300 ml pineapple juice	½ pint pineapple juice
700 g stewing lamb, trimmed and cut into 2½ cm pieces	1½ lb stewing lamb, trimmed and cut into 1 inch pieces
½–1 × 396 g can pineapple pieces	½–1 × 14 oz can pineapple pieces
25 g raisins	1 oz raisins
1 egg yolk	1 egg yolk
2 × 15 ml spoons milk	2 tablespoons milk

To garnish:
1 banana, thinly sliced

To garnish:
1 banana, thinly sliced

Cooking Time: 1½ hours
Oven: 160°C, 325°F, Gas Mark 3

Heat the butter in a frying pan and sauté the onions over a low heat, then stir in the curry powder and fry for a minute over a high heat, stir until blended, add the flour. Fry until coloured slightly, add the stock and stir well, then add drained pineapple juice. Turn into a casserole with the lamb, pineapple pieces, reserving a few for decoration, and raisins. Cover and cook until lamb is tender. When cooked remove from heat and add some stock to the beaten egg yolk and milk, return to hot casserole and stir until liquid thickens slightly. Taste and adjust seasoning. Serve on a bed of rice with sliced bananas dipped in lemon juice and a few pieces of pineapple.

Leek and lamb casserole

Metric	Imperial
700 g middle or best end neck of lamb	1½ lb middle or best end neck of lamb
50 g flour	2 oz flour
1 × 5 ml spoon salt	1 teaspoon salt
Freshly ground black pepper	Freshly ground black pepper
25 g cooking fat	1 oz cooking fat
3 leeks, coarsely sliced	3 leeks, coarsely sliced
396 g can tomatoes	14 oz can tomatoes
300 ml water or stock	½ pint water or stock
1 × 15 ml spoon tomato purée	1 tablespoon tomato purée
½ teaspoon dried thyme	½ teaspoon dried thyme
2 × 15 ml spoons mixed herbs	2 teaspoons mixed herbs

Cooking Time: 2¼ hours
Oven: 160°C, 325°F, Gas Mark 3

Toss lamb in flour seasoned with salt and pepper. Melt dripping in a large pan and fry the lamb on all sides to brown. Place in a casserole. Fry leeks gently for 2 minutes and place in the casserole with drained tomatoes, reserving juice. Add remaining flour to fat in the pan and cook for 1 minute. Stir in water or stock, juice from canned tomatoes, tomato purée, mixed chopped herbs and seasoning. Bring to the boil, stirring. Pour over lamb. Cover and cook in a moderate oven for 2 hours. Taste and adjust seasoning before serving.

Old time lamb; Noisettes in redcurrant jelly

Old time lamb

Metric

1 large breast of lamb,
boned
Salt and freshly ground
black pepper
50 g breadcrumbs
2 × 5 ml spoons parsley,
finely chopped
1 × 5 ml spoon chives,
finely chopped
1 × 5 ml spoon mint,
finely chopped
1 spring onion, washed
and chopped
6 canned apricot halves,
chopped
1 egg, beaten
2 × 15 ml spoons sherry
300 ml stock

To garnish:

Chopped spring onion
tops
Halved apricots

Imperial

1 large breast of lamb,
boned
Salt and freshly ground
black pepper
2 oz breadcrumbs
2 teaspoons parsley,
finely chopped
1 teaspoon chives,
finely chopped
1 teaspoon mint,
finely chopped
1 spring onion, washed
and chopped
6 canned apricot halves,
chopped
1 egg, beaten
2 tablespoons sherry
½ pint stock

To garnish:

Chopped spring onion
tops
Halved apricots

Cooking Time: 2 hours
Oven: 160°C, 325°F, Gas Mark 3

Lay out the breast of lamb and season well. Mix breadcrumbs, parsley, chives, mint, spring onion, apricots and
egg together, season well. Spread on to the lamb and roll up,
secure with skewers and brown under a high preheated grill
for several minutes. Place in a casserole. Pour over sherry
and stock, season well, cover and cook for 2 hours. Add
extra water or stock if necessary during cooking. Serve on a
heated dish, reduce stock in casserole to a glaze, pour over
the lamb and garnish with spring onion tops and halved
apricots

Oriental lamb

Noisettes in redcurrant jelly

Metric

8 noisettes of lamb
2 × 15 ml spoons
vegetable oil
Salt and freshly ground
black pepper
6 × 15 ml spoons
redcurrant jelly
3 × 15 ml spoons port

To garnish:
Watercress sprigs

Imperial

8 noisettes of lamb
2 tablespoons vegetable
oil
Salt and freshly ground
black pepper
6 tablespoons redcurrant
jelly
3 tablespoons port

To garnish:
Watercress sprigs

Cooking Time: 1 hour
Oven: 180°C, 350°F, Gas Mark 4

Brown the noisettes in the casserole for 2–3 minutes each
side in the oil. Season well and place redcurrant jelly on each
noisette. Pour port over the noisettes and cover. Cook for
1 hour in the oven. Remove and serve garnished with watercress sprigs.

Oriental lamb

Metric

450 g minced lamb
Salt and freshly ground
black pepper
¼ teaspoon mixed herbs
1 large onion, peeled and
sliced
2 × 15 ml spoons oil
1 leek, washed and sliced
1 aubergine, washed and
diced
396 g can tomatoes
1 cinnamon stick
Pinch ground coriander
Few cumin seeds
4 × 15 ml spoons water
150 ml white wine

Imperial

1 lb minced lamb
Salt and freshly ground
black pepper
¼ teaspoon mixed herbs
1 large onion, peeled and
sliced
2 tablespoons oil
1 leek, washed and sliced
1 aubergine, washed and
diced
14 oz can tomatoes
1 cinnamon stick
Pinch ground coriander
Few cumin seeds
4 tablespoons water
¼ pint white wine

Cooking Time: 1¼ hours
Oven: 160°C, 325°F, Gas Mark 3

Mix the lamb in a bowl with the seasoning and mixed herbs.
Make into small balls. Sauté the onion in oil until tender,
add the leek and leave pan on low heat. Coat the balls of
lamb with seasoned flour. Remove the leeks and onions to a
casserole and fry lamb until golden brown, lift into casserole. Place aubergine, tomatoes, cinnamon, herbs and
spices in the pan with the water and wine. Bring to the boil
and pour over the lamb. Cover and cook for one hour in the
oven. Taste and adjust seasoning before serving.

Orange lamb casserole

Orange lamb casserole

Metric	Imperial
2 × 15 ml spoons oil	2 tablespoons oil
1 kg stewing or shoulder of lamb, cut into cubes	2 lb stewing or shoulder of lamb, cut into cubes
1 × 5 ml spoon paprika	1 teaspoon paprika
15 g butter	½ oz butter
1 large onion, peeled and sliced	1 large onion, peeled and sliced
100 g mushrooms, washed and sliced	4 oz mushrooms, washed and sliced
150 ml water	¼ pint water
1 × 5 ml spoon horseradish sauce	1 teaspoon horseradish sauce
Pinch rosemary	Pinch rosemary
4–6 fresh mint leaves or ½ teaspoon dried	4–6 fresh mint leaves or ½ teaspoon dried
2 fresh leaves sage or ¼ teaspoon dried	2 fresh leaves sage or ¼ teaspoon dried
1 × 5 ml spoon salt	1 teaspoon salt
Freshly ground black pepper	Freshly ground black pepper
150 ml soured cream	¼ pint soured cream
Finely grated rind of 1 orange	Finely grated rind of 1 orange
3 × 15 ml spoons orange juice	3 tablespoons orange juice

Cooking Time: 1¼ hours
Oven: 180°C, 350°F, Gas Mark 4

Heat the oil, sprinkle lamb with paprika and brown in the frying pan. Cook until lamb is pale brown on all sides, remove to casserole. Add butter to pan, then sauté onion and mushrooms. Add the water, horseradish, herbs, salt and pepper and pour over lamb. Cover the casserole and cook for 1 hour or until the lamb is tender. Remove the meat and keep hot, add soured cream to onion mixture with grated orange rind and juice. Heat very gently, replace the meat, taste and adjust seasoning and serve.

Alternatively pour on soured cream before serving and sprinkle with grated orange rind and orange juice.

Lamb hot pot

Lamb hot pot

Metric

2 × 15 ml spoons oil
1 kg middle neck of lamb
or shoulder chops, cut into
2½ cm cubes
2 × 15 ml spoons
seasoned flour
450 g onions, peeled and
sliced
2 sticks celery, washed
and sliced
225 g carrots, peeled and
sliced
1 leek, washed and sliced
450 g potatoes, peeled and
sliced
300 ml stock
1 × 5 ml spoon
Worcestershire sauce
1 × 5 ml spoon rosemary,
finely chopped
Salt and freshly ground
black pepper
15 g butter

Imperial

2 tablespoons oil
2 lb middle neck of lamb
or shoulder chops, cut into
1 inch cubes
2 tablespoons seasoned
flour
1 lb onions, peeled and
sliced
2 sticks celery, washed
and sliced
8 oz carrots, peeled and
sliced
1 leek, washed and sliced
1 lb potatoes, peeled and
sliced
½ pint stock
1 teaspoon Worcestershire
sauce
1 teaspoon rosemary,
finely chopped
Salt and freshly ground
black pepper
½ oz butter

Cooking Time: 2¼ hours
Oven: 180°C, 350°F, Gas Mark 4

Heat the oil in a frying pan. Coat lamb in seasoned flour and brown in the oil. Add the onions and celery and reduce the heat for 5 minutes. Layer the lamb in a casserole with the onion mixture, carrots and leek, finishing with the potatoes. Pour in stock, Worcestershire sauce and rosemary. Season well. Dot with butter, cover and cook for 1¼ hours. Remove the lid for remaining 45 minutes of cooking time.

43

Sweet and sour lamb

Metric

1 breast of lamb, boned,
trimmed and cut into
2½ cm cubes
150 ml vinegar
150 ml stock or pineapple
juice
½ teaspoon salt
3 × 15 ml spoons brown
sugar
1 medium-sized onion,
sliced
227 g can pineapple
chunks
2 × 15 ml spoons
arrowroot

Imperial

1 breast lamb, boned,
trimmed and cut into
1 inch cubes
¼ pint vinegar
¼ pint stock or pineapple
juice
½ teaspoon salt
3 tablespoons brown sugar
1 medium-sized onion,
sliced
8 oz can pineapple
chunks
2 tablespoons arrowroot

Cooking Time: 2¼ hours
Oven: 180°C, 350°F, Gas Mark 4

Fry the lamb gently for 3–4 minutes. Place in a casserole, combine the other ingredients, except the arrowroot, and pour over lamb. Cover and bake in a moderate oven for 2 hours until tender. When cooked, skim off fat and thicken sauce with arrowroot. Taste and adjust the seasoning and serve with fried rice.

Lemon lamb casserole; Honeyed lamb

Sweet and sour lamb

Lemon lamb casserole

Metric	Imperial
450 g minced lamb	1 lb minced lamb
1 onion, peeled and finely chopped	1 onion, peeled and finely chopped
1 potato, peeled and grated	1 potato, peeled and grated
1 egg	1 egg
Salt and freshly ground black pepper	Salt and freshly ground black pepper
2 × 15 ml spoons finely chopped parsley	1 tablespoon finely chopped parsley
25 g flour	1 oz flour
25 g butter	1 oz butter
150 ml chicken stock	¼ pint chicken stock
Finely grated rind of 1 lemon	Finely grated rind of 1 lemon
2 × 15 ml spoons lemon juice	2 tablespoons lemon juice
2 eggs, beaten	2 eggs, beaten

Cooking Time: 45 minutes
Oven: 180°C, 350°F, Gas Mark 4

Put the minced lamb, onion, grated potato, egg, seasoning and parsley into a bowl and mix well. Form into small balls, roll in flour and allow to firm in the refrigerator. Heat the butter in a casserole and fry the floured lamb until golden brown. Pour in stock, add lemon rind and juice, bring to the boil, cover and cook for 30 minutes. Place lamb on a heated serving dish. Add the stock slowly and carefully to the beaten eggs and return to a very low heat to thicken. The mixture must not boil. Taste and adjust the seasoning and pour the egg mixture over the lamb. Garnish with lemon wedges and parsley.

Honeyed lamb

Metric	Imperial
2 × 15 ml spoons oil	2 tablespoons oil
2 potatoes, peeled and sliced	2 potatoes, peeled and sliced
1 large onion, peeled and sliced	1 large onion, peeled and sliced
2 sticks celery, washed and sliced	2 sticks celery, washed and sliced
1 kg breast of lamb, boned, rolled and tied	2 lb breast of lamb, boned, rolled and tied
Salt and freshly ground black pepper	Salt and freshly ground black pepper
2 × 5 ml spoons flour	2 teaspoons flour
1 orange	1 orange
2 × 15 ml spoons clear honey	2 tablespoons clear honey
300 ml chicken stock	½ pint chicken stock

Cooking Time: 1¾ hours
Oven: 180°C, 350°F, Gas Mark 4

Heat oil and sauté the vegetables for a few minutes and transfer to a casserole. Sprinkle breast of lamb with seasoning and flour and brown on all sides, place in casserole. Cut the orange in half and squeeze the juice from one half and grate a little rind from the squeezed skin. Mix the juice and rind with the honey, add the stock and pour over the breast of lamb. Season well and cover, cook for 1½ hours. Serve breast cut into slices garnished with orange butterflies and vegetables.

Leg of lamb, French style

Metric	Imperial
1 × 1½ kg leg of lamb	1 × 3½ lb leg of lamb
2 cloves garlic, peeled and thinly sliced	2 cloves garlic, peeled and thinly sliced
8 rosemary sprigs	8 rosemary sprigs
1 medium-sized onion, peeled and sliced	1 medium-sized onion, peeled and sliced
150 ml red wine	¼ pint red wine
150 ml stock	¼ pint stock
Salt and freshly ground black pepper	Salt and freshly ground black pepper
8 small potatoes, peeled	8 small potatoes, peeled
8 small carrots, peeled	8 small carrots, peeled
1 × 15 ml spoon flour	1 tablespoon flour

Cooking Time: 1½ hours
Oven: 180°C, 350°F, Gas Mark 4

Make small slits in the leg of lamb. Insert slices of garlic into slits, alternating with small sprigs of fresh rosemary. Arrange onion on the bottom of the casserole, place lamb on top. Pour on the wine and stock, season well, cover and put in the oven for 35 minutes. Cook the potatoes and carrots in boiling salted water for 5 minutes. Drain and sprinkle with salt and pepper, add to casserole, cook for a further 35 minutes. Remove lid of casserole for remaining 15 minutes, to allow meat to brown. Serve on a platter surrounded by vegetables. Pour off excess fat, if any, from gravy. Reduce on a high heat and sprinkle in flour, stir well to thicken slightly. Serve in a sauceboat separately.

Spiced Persian lamb

Metric	Imperial
450 g boneless shoulder of lamb, cut into 2½ cm cubes	1 lb boneless shoulder of lamb, cut into 1 inch cubes
1 small carton natural yogurt	1 small carton natural yogurt
4 cloves	4 cloves
4 black peppercorns	4 black peppercorns
2 small sticks cinnamon	2 small sticks cinnamon
1 × 5 ml spoon turmeric	1 teaspoon turmeric
4 large onions, finely sliced	4 large onions, finely sliced
100 g butter	4 oz butter
½ teaspoon paprika pepper	½ teaspoon paprika pepper
½ teaspoon chilli powder	½ teaspoon chilli powder
½ teaspoon curry powder	½ teaspoon curry powder
¼ teaspoon mixed spice	¼ teaspoon mixed spice
3–4 cumin seeds (optional)	3–4 cumin seeds (optional)
2–3 cardamoms (optional)	2–3 cardamoms (optional)
396 g can tomatoes	14 oz can tomatoes
300 ml stock	½ pint stock
2 potatoes, diced	2 potatoes, diced
Salt	Salt

Cooking Time: 1½ hours

Place the meat in a mixing bowl with the yogurt, 2 cloves, 2 peppercorns, one piece of cinnamon and half the turmeric. Mix well and leave for at least 2 hours. Fry the onions in the butter until golden brown. Add the remaining spices and fry for a few minutes. Add the meat and cook, stirring, over a moderate heat for 5 minutes. Add the tomatoes, stock and potatoes and stir well. Cover and simmer for 1–1¼ hours, until the lamb is tender. Taste and adjust seasoning and serve with boiled rice. Garnish, if liked, with tomato wedges and parsley.

Leg of lamb, French style; Spiced Persian lamb

As pork animals are usually young, most cuts are tender and can be cooked by any method. Less time is therefore required for pork casseroles to tenderise the meat than for beef and lamb stewing cuts. Ham and pork casseroles can add variety to every day menus and ham is especially good to add flavour to veal casseroles. A slice or two of bacon is often used to flavour other meat and poultry casseroles. Choose pork with firm, smooth flesh without gristle and a light marbling of fat. Flesh should never be grey and soft. Good quality animals have a thick layer of fat on the outside.

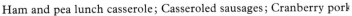

Ham and pea lunch casserole; Casseroled sausages; Cranberry pork

Ham and pea lunch casserole

Metric	Imperial
700 g bacon hock, trimmed and cubed	1½ lb bacon hock, trimmed and cubed
1 × 15 ml spoon oil	1 tablespoon oil
1 onion, peeled and sliced	1 onion, peeled and sliced
396 g can ham and pea soup	14 oz can ham and pea soup
Freshly ground pepper	Freshly ground pepper
2 potatoes, peeled and diced	2 potatoes, peeled and diced
Sprig of thyme or ¼ teaspoon dried	Sprig of thyme or ¼ teaspoon dried
100 g frozen peas	4 oz frozen peas

Cooking Time: 1¾ hours
Oven: 180°C, 350°F, Gas Mark 2

If bacon is unpackaged, soak for several hours in cold water. Pre-packed joints tend to be less salty, therefore soaking is unnecessary. Heat oil, sauté the onion gently for 2 minutes, then add the cubed bacon and cook for 3–4 minutes. Place the bacon and onion in a casserole with the ham and pea soup, pepper, potato and thyme. Cover and cook for 1½ hours. Stir in the peas 15 minutes before cooking has finished. Taste and adjust seasoning.

Cranberry pork

Metric	Imperial
2 × 15 ml spoons oil	2 tablespoons oil
1 × 1½ kg rolled shoulder of pork	1 × 3½ lb rolled shoulder of pork
225 g cranberries	8 oz cranberries
150 ml water	¼ pint water
Salt and freshly ground black pepper	Salt and freshly ground black pepper
2 × 15 ml spoons honey	2 tablespoons honey
1 × 5 ml spoon finely grated orange rind	1 teaspoon finely grated orange rind
Pinch of ground cloves	Pinch of ground cloves
Pinch of ground nutmeg	Pinch of ground nutmeg

Cooking Time: 1¾ hours
Oven: 180°C, 350°F, Gas Mark 4

Heat the oil and brown the pork in a frying pan on all sides. Cook the cranberries for 5 minutes in the water after it has boiled. Transfer the pork to the casserole, season well and spread with honey and grated orange rind. Sprinkle with cloves and nutmeg, pour in cranberries, cover and cook for 1½ hours. Taste and adjust seasoning. Serve sliced with the sauce.

Casseroled sausages

Metric	Imperial
4 large pork sausages with herbs	4 large pork sausages with herbs
4 thick rashers bacon, rinded	4 thick rashers bacon, rinded
1 onion, peeled and chopped	1 onion, peeled and chopped
25 g butter	1 oz butter
2 × 15 ml spoons oil	2 tablespoons oil
1½ × 5 ml spoons dried sage	1½ teaspoons dried sage
1½ × 15 ml spoons flour	1½ tablespoons flour
450 ml stock	¾ pint stock
Salt and freshly ground black pepper	Salt and freshly ground black pepper
150 ml soured cream	¼ pint soured cream
225 g noodles	8 oz noodles
25 g butter	1 oz butter
Pinch nutmeg	Pinch nutmeg
To garnish:	To garnish:
2 × 15 ml spoons finely chopped parsley	2 tablespoons finely chopped parsley

Cooking Time: 40 minutes

Roll up each sausage in a rasher of bacon, and tie round with thick cotton or fine string to secure. Fry the onion gently in the butter and oil for 5 minutes. Add the sage and the tied sausages and fry for 5 minutes. Remove the sausages to a plate. Stir the flour into the fat remaining in the pan and cook for 1 minute. Gradually stir in the stock. Bring to the boil and add seasoning and soured cream. Return sausages and stock to casserole. Cover and simmer for 20 minutes. taste and adjust the seasoning. Cook the noodles in a large saucepan of boiling salted water for about 8 minutes. Drain and toss in butter with a pinch of nutmeg and pepper. Serve sausages with cooked noodles, sprinkled with chopped parsley.

49

Honeyed shoulder of pork with red cabbage

Metric	Imperial
2 × 15 ml spoons oil	2 tablespoons oil
1¼ kg shoulder of pork	3 lb shoulder of pork
15 g butter	½ oz butter
2 small onions, peeled and sliced	2 small onions, peeled and sliced
1 small red cabbage, washed and shredded	1 small red cabbage, washed and shredded
150 ml red wine	¼ pint red wine
150 ml stock	¼ pint stock
Salt and freshly ground black pepper	Salt and freshly ground black pepper
2 × 15 ml spoons honey	2 tablespoons honey

Cooking Time: 1½–1¾ hours
Oven: 180°C, 350°F, Gas Mark 4

Heat the oil in a frying pan and brown the pork on all sides. Remove from pan. Add the butter and sauté the onions. transfer to a casserole. Blanch the cabbage by placing it in boiling water for about 3 minutes. Drain well and place in the casserole with the onions. Pour over the red wine and stock and season well. Spread the honey over the skin of the pork and place on the vegetable mixture. Cover and cook in the oven for 1½ hours. Taste and adjust seasoning.

Hawaiian pork casserole

Metric	Imperial
450 g pork, cubed	1 lb pork, cubed
432 g can pineapple chunks	15¼ oz can pineapple chunks
Salt and freshly ground black pepper	Salt and freshly ground black pepper
½ teaspoon allspice	½ teaspoon allspice
3 × 15 ml spoons oil	3 tablespoons oil
1 onion, peeled and finely chopped	1 onion, peeled and finely chopped
1 green pepper, seeded and sliced	1 green pepper, seeded and sliced
3 × 15 ml spoons seasoned flour	3 tablespoons seasoned flour
150 ml stock	¼ pint stock
1 × 15 ml spoon sherry	1 tablespoon sherry
1 × 15 ml spoon cornflour	1 tablespoon cornflour
To garnish:	To garnish:
Strips of green pepper	Strips of green pepper

Cooking Time: 1 hour
Oven: 160°C, 325°F, Gas Mark 3

Marinate the pork in the pineapple juice with seasoning and allspice, for 1 hour. Heat 1 × 15 ml spoon (1 tablespoon) of the oil and sauté the onion and green pepper for 5 minutes. Transfer the vegetables to a casserole. Drain the pork, dip in seasoned flour and fry in the remaining oil until golden brown. Place in the casserole with the marinade, stock and sherry. Cover and put in the oven to cook. After 45 minutes thicken the gravy with the cornflour and add the pineapple chunks. Taste and adjust the seasoning. Serve garnished with strips of raw green pepper.

Spanish pork chops

Metric	Imperial
4 rashers smoked bacon, rinded and chopped	4 rashers smoked bacon, rinded and chopped
1 × 15 ml spoon oil	1 tablespoon oil
1 onion, peeled and chopped	1 onion, peeled and chopped
4 pork chops, with kidneys	4 pork chops, with kidneys
1 × 15 ml spoon flour	1 tablespoon flour
Salt and freshly ground black pepper	Salt and freshly ground black pepper
150 ml red wine	¼ pint red wine
1 × 15 ml spoon tomato purée	1 tablespoon tomato purée
20 stuffed olives, sliced	20 stuffed olives, sliced
To garnish:	To garnish:
2 hard-boiled eggs, sliced	2 hard-boiled eggs, sliced

Cooking Time: 35 minutes
Oven: 190°C, 375°F, Gas Mark 5

Fry the bacon, remove to a casserole, add oil to frying pan. Sauté onion for a few minutes and transfer to the casserole. Dust the chops with seasoned flour and fry on both sides to brown and place in the casserole on the bacon and onions. Mix wine with tomato purée and pour over chops. Cover and cook for 25 minutes, then add the olives and cook for a further 5 minutes. Garnish with slices of hard-boiled egg with a slice of olive in the centre.

Hawaiian pork casserole; Honeyed shoulder of pork with red cabbage; Spanish pork chops

Sweet and sour pork

Metric	Imperial
1 × 15 ml spoon oil	1 tablespoon oil
1 × 15 ml spoon sherry	1 tablespoon sherry
1 × 15 ml spoon honey	1 tablespoon honey
2 × 15 ml spoons vinegar	2 tablespoons vinegar
1 × 15 ml spoon soy sauce	1 tablespoon soy sauce
Salt and freshly ground black pepper	Salt and freshly ground black pepper
450 g pork, cubed	1 lb pork, cubed
2 × 15 ml spoons oil	2 tablespoons oil
1 onion, peeled and diced	1 onion, peeled and diced
2 carrots, peeled and diced	2 carrots, peeled and diced
1 green pepper, seeded and diced	1 green pepper, seeded and diced
50 g mushrooms, washed and sliced	2 oz mushrooms, washed and sliced
300 ml stock	$\frac{1}{2}$ pint stock
1 × 15 ml spoon soy sauce	1 tablespoon soy sauce
269 g can bean sprouts, drained	$9\frac{1}{4}$ oz can bean sprouts, drained
1 × 15 ml spoon cornflour	1 tablespoon cornflour

Cooking Time: 1 hour
Oven: 160°C, 325°F, Gas Mark 3

Mix the oil, sherry, honey, vinegar and soy sauce in a bowl and season well. Marinate the pork in the mixture for at least 2 hours, turning from time to time. Heat 1 × 15 ml spoon (1 tablespoon) oil and fry the onion, carrots, pepper and mushrooms. Place in a casserole. Drain the pork and brown in the remaining oil. Transfer to the casserole and add the marinade, stock, seasoning and remaining soy sauce. Cover and cook for $\frac{1}{2}$ hour, then add the bean sprouts. After 15 minutes thicken the liquid with cornflour and return to cook for the remaining 15 minutes. Taste and adjust the seasoning.

Lemon and lime pork

Metric	Imperial
25 g butter	1 oz butter
1 clove garlic, peeled and crushed	1 clove garlic, peeled and crushed
2 onions, peeled and chopped	2 onions, peeled and chopped
450 g leg of pork, cut into $1\frac{1}{4}$ cm pieces	1 lb leg of pork, cut into $\frac{1}{2}$ inch pieces
Finely grated rind of 1 lemon	Finely grated rind of 1 lemon
2 × 15 ml spoons lime juice	2 tablespoons lime juice
150 ml water	$\frac{1}{4}$ pint water
2 × 15 ml spoons single cream	2 tablespoons single cream
1 egg yolk	1 egg yolk
Salt and freshly ground black pepper	Salt and freshly ground black pepper

To garnish:
Lemon or lime slices

Cooking Time: 1 hour
Oven: 190°C, 375°F, Gas Mark 5

Heat the butter, add garlic and onions and sauté for a few minutes, transfer to a small casserole. Fry the pork for about 3 minutes, add to the casserole with lemon rind, lime juice and water, cover and cook for 40 minutes. Place pork in a heated dish. Mix the cream and the egg, season well and pour in some of the lime juice mixture, beat well, add remaining liquid, return to heat until sauce thickens. Taste and adjust the seasoning. Garnish with slices of lime or lemon. Serve with mashed potatoes.

52

Spare ribs

Metric

1½ kg Chinese-style spare
ribs
4 × 15 ml spoons soy
sauce
2 × 15 ml spoons orange
marmalade
1 clove garlic, crushed
1 large onion, peeled and
sliced
Salt and freshly ground
black pepper
300 ml stock or water
1 × 15 ml spoon vinegar

Imperial

3 lb Chinese-style spare
ribs
4 tablespoons soy sauce
2 tablespoons orange
marmalade
1 clove garlic, crushed
1 large onion, peeled and
sliced
Salt and freshly ground
black pepper
½ pint stock or water
1 tablespoon vinegar

Cooking Time : 1¾ hours
Oven : 200°C, 400°F, Gas Mark 6

Brown the spare ribs under a high grill. Mix the soya sauce,
marmalade, and crushed garlic together and spread over
the ribs. Place sliced onion on the bottom of a casserole,
place ribs on top, season well. Pour over stock and vinegar.
Cover and cook for 1½ hours. Remove lid to allow to crisp
before serving. Taste and adjust the seasoning.

Pork fillet veronique; Stuffed pork chops

Spare ribs

Stuffed pork chops

Metric	Imperial
4 thick pork chops	4 thick pork chops
25 g breadcrumbs	1 oz breadcrumbs
1 × 5 ml spoon dried sage	1 teaspoon dried sage
1 small onion, peeled and finely chopped	1 small onion, peeled and finely chopped
25 g sultanas	1 oz sultanas
Finely grated rind of $\frac{1}{2}$ lemon	Finely grated rind of $\frac{1}{2}$ lemon
$\frac{1}{2}$ egg, beaten	$\frac{1}{2}$ egg, beaten
Salt and freshly ground black pepper	Salt and freshly ground black pepper
300 ml cider	$\frac{1}{2}$ pint cider
To garnish:	To garnish:
1 × 15 ml spoon finely chopped parsley	1 tablespoon finely chopped parsley

Cooking Time: 1 hour
Oven: 180°C, 350°F, Gas Mark 4

Cut a slit in the skin of each chop to allow a pocket for stuffing. Brown the chops on each side quickly under a preheated grill. Mix the breadcrumbs, sage, onion, sultanas and lemon rind in a bowl with the egg, season well. Stuff into the chops, arrange in a casserole and season well. Pour over cider, cover and cook in the oven. Serve on a heated dish, garnished with chopped parsley. Cider sauce may be thickened with cornflour and served separately.
Alternatively eight thin chops may be used, sandwich two with stuffing between and secure with a wooden cocktail stick. Serve on a hot dish, garnished with chopped parsley or watercress.

Pork fillet veronique

Metric	Imperial
2 pork fillets, trimmed	2 pork fillets, trimmed
24 green grapes, halved and seeded	24 green grapes, halved and seeded
50 g butter	2 oz butter
150 ml white wine	$\frac{1}{4}$ pint white wine
150 ml chicken stock	$\frac{1}{4}$ pint chicken stock
Salt and freshly ground black pepper	Salt and freshly ground black pepper
1 onion, peeled and quartered	1 onion, peeled and quartered
1 carrot, peeled and sliced	1 carrot, peeled and sliced
1 bay leaf	1 bay leaf
$\frac{1}{4}$ teaspoon or sprig of thyme	$\frac{1}{4}$ teaspoon or sprig of thyme
25 g butter	1 oz butter
25 g flour	1 oz flour
1 egg yolk	1 egg yolk

Cooking Time: $1\frac{1}{4}$ hours
Oven: 180°C, 350°F, Gas Mark 4

Cut the pork fillets halfway through and open out. Stuff 12 halved grapes with a knob of butter and arrange down the centre of one fillet, place the other on top to form a roll and tie with string. Heat some butter and brown fillet on all sides, transfer to a casserole, add wine, stock, seasoning, onion and carrot, bay leaf and thyme. Cover and cook for 1 hour. Place pork on a heated serving plate, remove string. Heat the butter until it is slightly brown and quickly add the flour, cook roux until blond, add strained liquid from the casserole. Mix the beaten egg yolk with a little sauce then return to remainder of sauce on a low heat to thicken, taste and adjust seasoning. Pour over fillets and decorate with remaining halved grapes.

Gammon steaks with pineapple

Metric

4 gammon steaks
16 cloves
4 × 5 ml spoons brown sugar
Freshly ground black pepper
396 g can pineapple rings
2 tomatoes, halved
1 × 15 ml spoon cornflour

Imperial

4 gammon steaks
16 cloves
4 teaspoons brown sugar
Freshly ground black pepper
14 oz can pineapple rings
2 tomatoes, halved
1 tablespoon cornflour

Cooking Time: 50 minutes
Oven: 180°C, 350°F, Gas Mark 3

Snip gammon fat with scissors to avoid shrinking, stick cloves into the steaks, sprinkle with brown sugar, and pepper. Pour over the pineapple juice and bake for 40 minutes in a casserole. Uncover, pour off the juice, place a pineapple ring on each steak, top with a halved tomato and replace in the oven to heat through. Thicken the juice by adding cornflour mixed in a little water, taste and adjust the seasoning and pour over pineapple and gammon. Serve with creamed potatoes.

Mediterranean pork

Metric

4 pork chops, thinly cut
25 g plain flour
Salt and freshly ground black pepper
1 × 15 ml spoon oil
100 g can mushrooms or 100 g mushrooms, cooked in water and liquid retained
3 × 15 ml spoons tomato purée
1 small onion, peeled and sliced
½ green pepper, seeded and sliced
1 clove garlic, crushed

Imperial

4 pork chops, thinly cut
1 oz plain flour
Salt and freshly ground black pepper
1 tablespoon oil
4 oz can mushrooms or 4 oz mushrooms, cooked in water and liquid retained
3 tablespoons tomato purée
1 small onion, peeled and sliced
½ green pepper, seeded and sliced
1 clove garlic, crushed

Cooking Time: 1 hour
Oven: 160°C, 325°F, Gas Mark 3

Dip the chops in seasoned flour. Brown quickly, on both sides in the oil. Place the liquid from the mushrooms in goblet of a liquidiser together with tomato purée, onion, pepper and garlic and blend for 20 seconds. Pour half into a casserole and add the pork chops and mushrooms, then the remaining tomato mixture. Cover and bake for 40 minutes. Uncover and continue cooking for another 20 minutes.

Braised ham

Metric

1 kg forehock or middle gammon
300 ml pale ale
Freshly ground black pepper
2 × 15 ml spoons honey
4 × 15 ml spoons Demerara sugar
1 × 5 ml spoon dry mustard
12 cloves

Imperial

2¼ lb forehock or middle gammon
½ pint pale ale
Freshly ground black pepper
2 tablespoons honey
4 tablespoons Demerara sugar
1 teaspoon dry mustard
12 cloves

Cooking Time: 1 hour 10 minutes
Oven: 180°C, 350°F, Gas Mark 4
        200°C, 400°F, Gas Mark 6

Soak the ham in cold water for several hours. Drain and place in a casserole with pale ale and cook, sprinkled with pepper and covered, for 40 minutes. Remove and discard half the ale. Remove the skin and score the fat diagonally with a sharp knife. Mix honey, sugar and dry mustard together and rub over the ham. Stud diamond shapes on the skin with cloves and return ham to the oven, without lid, and with half the ale, for a further 30 minutes at the higher temperature. Baste every 10 minutes.

Gammon steak with pineapple; Mediterranean pork; Braised ham

There are two types of veal on the market, milk fed veal which often comes from Holland, and grass fed which is less tender but can have more flavour and is less expensive. Veal should be firm and moist, never flabby, always avoid mottled flesh which is dark and dry looking.
Cuts of veal suitable for the casserole: Middle neck, Knuckle, Scrag, Shoulder, Breast and Leg.
Veal bones are pink and white and as they come from a young animal they are soft, and produce excellent white stock and jelly when boiled.
To make Veal stock place the cut up veal bones in $1\frac{1}{4}$ l ($2\frac{1}{4}$ pints) of water with 1 onion, 1 carrot, bay leaf and some peppercorns, bring to the boil and simmer until there is approximately 1 l ($1\frac{3}{4}$ pints) left.

Veal casserole; Sweet pepper casserole

Veal casserole

Metric	Imperial
1 kg veal, trimmed and cut into 2½ cm cubes	*2 lb veal, trimmed and cut into 1 inch cubes*
3 × 15 ml spoons oil	*3 tablespoons oil*
50 g butter	*2 oz butter*
3 medium-sized onions, peeled and cut into rings	*3 medium-sized onions, peeled and cut into rings*
150 ml dry white wine	*¼ pint dry white wine*
1 green pepper, seeded and diced	*1 green pepper, seeded and diced*
2 carrots, peeled and sliced	*2 carrots, peeled and sliced*
396 g can peeled tomatoes	*14 oz can peeled tomatoes*
½ teaspoon marjoram	*½ teaspoon marjoram*
½ teaspoon paprika	*½ teaspoon paprika*
Salt and freshly ground black pepper	*Salt and freshly ground black pepper*
150 ml beef stock	*¼ pint beef stock*
4 rashers of bacon, or 100 g belly of pork, cut into 1¼ cm cubes	*4 rashers of bacon, or 4 oz belly of pork, cut into ½ inch cubes*
100 g mushrooms, washed and sliced	*4 oz mushrooms, washed and sliced*
150 ml soured cream	*¼ pint soured cream*

To garnish:
1 × 15 ml spoon finely chopped chives or parsley

To garnish:
1 tablespoon finely chopped chives or parsley

Cooking Time: 1½ hours

Dredge the veal with flour and brown in a frying pan in the oil and butter, add onions and sauté until tender, about 5 minutes. Fry bacon or belly of pork until lightly brown, add to the veal and onions. Pour in wine, mix with meat and onions and place in a heavy-based saucepan. Add pepper, carrots and tomatoes. Cover and simmer for 10 minutes. Add herbs, seasoning and stock. Bring to the boil, then simmer for 45 minutes. Add sliced mushrooms and simmer for another 20 minutes.

Remove from heat and stir in soured cream. Taste and adjust the seasoning and serve sprinkled with chopped chives or parsley.

Sweet pepper casserole

Metric	Imperial
4 veal cutlets	*4 veal cutlets*
450 g onions, peeled and chopped	*1 lb onions, peeled and chopped*
50 g butter	*2 oz butter*
1 × 15 ml spoon oil	*1 tablespoon oil*
1 green pepper, seeded and cut into strips	*1 green pepper, seeded and cut into strips*
396 g can tomatoes	*14 oz can tomatoes*
½ teaspoon caster sugar	*½ teaspoon caster sugar*
1 chicken stock cube	*1 chicken stock cube*
Salt and freshly ground black pepper	*Salt and freshly ground black pepper*
Pinch of marjoram	*Pinch of marjoram*
4 new potatoes, peeled and sliced into rounds	*4 new potatoes, peeled and sliced in rounds*

Cooking Time: 40 minutes
Oven: 180°C, 350°F, Gas Mark 4

Place the cutlets under a hot grill for 5 minutes, turning once. Place in a casserole and keep hot. To make the sauce, fry the onions in the butter and oil until transparent. Add the pepper, tomatoes, sugar and the stock cube, dissolved in 150 ml (¼ pint) boiling water, and seasoning. Add to the casserole with the potatoes, cover and place in a moderate oven for 30 minutes. Taste and adjust the seasoning. Serve with new potatoes and sliced green beans.

VEAL
Veal rolls

Metric

75 g bacon
50 g suet
75 g breadcrumbs
Rind of ½ lemon, finely grated
¼ teaspoon mixed herbs
Salt and freshly ground black pepper
Beaten egg
4 slices leg of veal, thinly cut
25 g flour
50 g fat
2 small onions, peeled and sliced
1 carrot, peeled and sliced
600 ml water or stock
2 × 15 ml spoons tomato purée

To garnish:
Finely chopped parsley

Imperial

3 oz bacon
2 oz suet
3 oz breadcrumbs
Rind of ½ lemon, finely grated
¼ teaspoon mixed herbs
Salt and freshly ground black pepper
Beaten egg
4 slices leg of veal, thinly cut
1 oz flour
2 oz fat
2 small onions, peeled and sliced
1 carrot, peeled and sliced
1 pint water or stock
2 tablespoons tomato purée

To garnish:
Finely chopped parsley

Cooking Time: 1¾ hours
Oven: 180°C, 350°F, Gas Mark 4

Chop the bacon finely, add all the stuffing ingredients and bind with the beaten egg. Beat the veal to flatten, with a rolling pin. Spread with the stuffing and roll up and tie with fine string, toss in seasoned flour. Heat the fat in a casserole, fry meat to brown lightly, drain and remove. Fry sliced onion and carrot and any flour left, for 1–2 minutes. Add stock or water and tomato purée, taste and adjust seasoning. Put in veal rolls, cover and simmer gently for 1½ hours or until meat is tender. Sprinkle with parsley before serving or garnish with watercress.

Veal rolls

Veal paprika

Metric

450 g pie veal, trimmed
of fat and cubed
1 × 15 ml spoon flour
1 × 15 ml spoon paprika
Salt and freshly ground
black pepper
25 g margarine
1 onion, peeled and sliced
150 ml stock
2 sticks celery, washed
and chopped
225 g tomatoes, skinned
seeded and chopped
1 × 15 ml spoon tomato
purée
1 × 15 ml spoon finely
chopped parsley
Paprika
3 × 15 ml spoons soured
cream

Imperial

1 lb pie veal, trimmed of
fat and cubed
1 tablespoon flour
1 tablespoon paprika
Salt and freshly ground
black pepper
1 oz margarine
1 onion, peeled and sliced
¼ pint stock
2 sticks celery, washed
and chopped
8 oz tomatoes, skinned,
seeded and chopped
1 tablespoon tomato
purée
1 tablespoon finely
chopped parsley
Paprika
3 tablespoons soured
cream

Cooking Time: 1¾–2 hours
Oven: 180°C, 350°F, Gas Mark 4

Toss the veal in flour, paprika and seasoning. Heat margarine gently in a large frying pan. Add the veal and fry with the onion for 5 minutes. Stir in the stock and bring to the boil, stirring. Add celery, tomatoes and purée. Transfer to a casserole. Cover and bake on the middle shelf of the oven for 1½–1¾ hours until meat is tender. Taste and adjust the seasoning. Sprinkle with chopped parsley and paprika, and pour over soured cream.

Veal paprika

I prefer the American name of 'variety meats' for these delicious and nutritious parts of the animal. Most offal has very little waste and is therefore reasonably economical. Always eat offal fresh and if pre-packed, unwrap and store in the refrigerator until it is to be cooked. Do not store offal in airtight polythene containers.

The following offal is suitable for the casserole

Lambs' Brains can be used with the head for stews, but are expensive now.

Ox Cheek is very economical and is excellent after long slow cooking in a casserole.

Lambs' Tongue may be braised in a casserole.

Pigs Head can be cooked in a casserole for brawn.

Heart – Ox, Calfs' and Lambs' are also excellent with long, slow cooking in a casserole.

Kidneys – Ox, Calf, Lamb and Pig can all be used in casserole dishes.

Liver – Ox, Lambs' and Pigs' are all suitable for casseroles.

Oxtail. Excellent after long, slow cooking in the casserole.

Lamb kidneys in Cinzano

Metric

8 lamb's kidneys, cleaned and skinned
225 g mushrooms, washed
2 × 5 ml spoons lemon juice
25 g butter
Salt and freshly ground black pepper
75 ml Cinzano (white)
2 × 15 ml spoons cream (optional)

To garnish:
2 × 15 ml spoons finely chopped parsley

Imperial

8 lamb's kidneys, cleaned and skinned
8 oz mushrooms, washed
2 teaspoons lemon juice
1 oz butter
Salt and freshly ground black pepper
$\frac{1}{8}$ pint Cinzano (white)
2 tablespoons cream (optional)

To garnish:
2 tablespoons finely chopped parsley

Cooking Time: 25 minutes
Oven: 160°C, 325°F, Gas Mark 3

Cut the kidneys in half, remove the core and slice again. Slice the mushrooms lengthwise down the stalks and sprinkle with lemon juice. Heat the butter in a frying pan, sauté the kidneys, then add the mushrooms to cook for about 3 minutes. Season well and arrange in a casserole. Pour over the Cinzano, cover and cook in the oven for 20 minutes. Taste and adjust the seasoning. Sprinkle with cream and serve garnished with parsley.

Oxtail with sausages

Metric

2 oxtails
50 g lard
1 large onion, peeled and sliced
600 ml stock
150 ml white wine
Bouquet garni
Salt and freshly ground black pepper
4 sausages

Beurre manié
25 g butter mixed with
1 × 15 ml spoon plain flour
1 × 5 ml spoon Worcestershire sauce

To garnish:
Parsley

Imperial

2 oxtails
2 oz lard
1 large onion, peeled and sliced
1 pint stock
$\frac{1}{4}$ pint white wine
Bouquet garni
Salt and freshly ground black pepper
4 sausages

Beurre manié
1 oz butter mixed with
1 tablespoon plain flour
1 teaspoon Worcestershire sauce

To garnish:
Parsley

Cooking Time: 3 hours
Oven: 160°C, 325°F, Gas Mark 3

Brown the oxtails in lard, together with the onion. Drain and transfer to a casserole. Add the stock, wine, bouquet garni and seasoning. Cover and cook in the oven until tender. Remove the meat from the bones and keep warm. Remove bouquet garni. Skim the fat from the cooled sauce. Cook the sausages until nicely browned and cut each into half. Arrange round the meat on a serving dish. Thicken the sauce with the beurre manié, add the Worcestershire sauce and seasoning, if necessary. Pour over the meat. Garnish with parsley and serve surrounded by a border of mashed potato.

Oxtail with sausages; Lamb kidneys in cinzano

Oxtail casserole

Metric	Imperial
2 oxtails, cut into 5 cm pieces	2 oxtails, cut into 2 inch pieces
2 × 15 ml spoons oil	2 tablespoons oil
2 medium-sized onions, peeled and sliced	2 medium-sized onions, peeled and sliced
2 medium-sized carrots, peeled and sliced	2 medium-sized carrots, peeled and sliced
1 clove garlic, crushed	1 clove garlic, crushed
2 × 15 ml spoons tomato purée	2 tablespoons tomato purée
300 ml stock	½ pint stock
150 ml sherry	¼ pint sherry
Salt and freshly ground black pepper	Salt and freshly ground black pepper
Bouquet garni	Bouquet garni
450 g button onions, peeled	1 lb button onions, peeled
100 g button mushrooms, washed	4 oz button mushrooms, washed
25 g butter	1 oz butter

Cooking Time: 2½ hours
Oven: 160°C, 325°F, Gas Mark 3

Brown the oxtail in the oil. Remove to a casserole. Sauté the vegetables and put on top of the oxtail. Blend the tomato purée, stock and sherry. Pour over the contents of the casserole. Season and add bouquet garni. Cover and cook for 2 hours. Remove bouquet garni. Remove meat from the bones and skim the fat from the cooled sauce. Return meat to the casserole and keep warm. Sauté the onions for 10 minutes, add mushrooms and continue cooking for a further 7 minutes. Add to the meat. Simmer together for 10 minutes. Taste and adjust the seasoning before serving.

Brawn

Metric	Imperial
½ pig's head	½ pig's head
2 l cold water	3½ pints cold water
2 onions, peeled and quartered	2 onions, peeled and quartered
1 carrot, peeled and halved	1 carrot, peeled and halved
1 turnip, peeled and quartered	1 turnip, peeled and quartered
4 cloves	4 cloves
12 peppercorns	12 peppercorns
1 blade of mace	1 blade of mace
Bouquet garni	Bouquet garni
Salt and freshly ground black pepper	Salt and freshly ground black pepper

To garnish:
Slices of hard-boiled egg or tomato

To garnish:
Slices of hard-boiled egg or tomato

Cooking Time: 3¼ hours
Oven: 160°C, 325°F, Gas Mark 3

This recipe is included as it is delicious and many people have pigs' heads when buying pork for the freezer. Prepare it in a large casserole to cut down smells in the kitchen. Wash the head thoroughly in tepid water, remove gristle and soft nostrils then rinse thoroughly in cold water. Place the head into a large casserole with enough cold water to cover, bring to the boil slowly. Skim carefully then add the vegetables, herbs and bouquet garni. Cover and place in the oven, remove lid and skim after the first and second hours. At the end of 3 hours the flesh should come easily away from the bones. Strain the liquid into a basin and place head on a dish, allow to cool. Cut tongue and meat from head into pieces, removing all skin, gristle and fat. Place liquid and bones into a pot and boil until it is reduced by half, season well. Place meat in a mould and pour in juice. This will set into a firm jelly and can be turned out on to a bed of salad and garnish with hard-boiled egg or tomato slices.

Brawn; Oxtail casserole

Tripe and onions

Metric	Imperial
1000 g tripe	2½ lb tripe
300 ml milk	½ pint milk
300 ml water	½ pint water
4 large onions, peeled and thickly sliced	4 large onions, peeled and thickly sliced
Salt and freshly ground black pepper	Salt and freshly ground black pepper
25 g cornflour	1 oz cornflour

Cooking Time: 2½–3½ hours
Oven: 150°C, 300°F, Gas Mark 2

Cut tripe into strips. Bring milk and water to the boil in a casserole. Add the tripe and onions. Season, cover and simmer gently for 2½ hours or cook in the oven for 3½ hours. Remove. Thicken the sauce with cornflour and simmer for a few minutes.

Lambs' hearts with celery and apple

Metric	Imperial
450 g lambs' hearts washed and thinly sliced	1 lb lambs' hearts, washed and thinly sliced
1 large onion, peeled and sliced	1 large onion, peeled and sliced
50 g lard	2 oz lard
6 sticks celery, washed and sliced	6 sticks celery, washed and sliced
15 g butter	½ oz butter
15 g cornflour	½ oz cornflour
300 ml stock	½ pint stock
1 × 15 ml spoon tomato purée	1 tablespoon tomato purée
4 × 15 ml spoons red wine (optional)	4 tablespoons red wine (optional)
Bouquet garni	Bouquet garni
Salt and freshly ground black pepper	Salt and freshly ground black pepper
225 g red skinned apples, washed, cored and sliced	8 oz red skinned apples, washed, cored and sliced

Cooking Time: 2¼ hours
Oven: 160°C, 325°F, Gas Mark 3

Brown the heart slices and onion in the lard. Place in a casserole. Sauté the celery in the butter. Place in the casserole. Add the cornflour to the butter to make a roux; blend in the stock, purée and red wine and cook well. Add to the casserole with the bouquet garni and seasoning. Arrange sliced apples on top. Cover and cook for 2 hours. Remove bouquet garni. Taste and adjust the seasoning before serving.

Braised tongue and Madeira

Metric	Imperial
1¼–1½ kg tongue	2½–3 lb tongue
1 large onion, peeled and sliced	1 large onion, peeled and sliced
1 large carrot, peeled and sliced	1 large carrot, peeled and sliced
1 bay leaf	1 bay leaf
1 teaspoon thyme	½ teaspoon thyme
6 peppercorns, roughly crushed	6 peppercorns, roughly crushed
Salt and freshly ground black pepper	Salt and freshly ground black pepper
25 g butter	1 oz butter
25 g flour	1 oz flour
150 ml Madeira	¼ pint Madeira

Cooking Time: 3½–3¾ hours
Oven: 150°C, 300°F, Gas Mark 2

Place the tongue, vegetables, herbs and peppercorns in a saucepan with enough hot water to cover. Bring to the boil, cover with the lid and simmer gently for 3 hours until tender. Remove the tongue, cut away the root and skin. Cut into slices and place in a casserole. Make a brown roux by melting the butter until it is foaming and turns golden on a high heat, add the flour and allow to brown. Add 300 ml (½ pint) of cooking liquid and cook until smooth and pale brown. Sieve if necessary, add the Madeira and cook for about 2 minutes. Pour over the sliced tongue in the casserole. Cover and return to the oven for 30 minutes.

Lambs' hearts with celery and apple; Braised tongue and Madeira; Tripe and onions

Stuffed liver casserole

Metric	Imperial
¾ kg liver (about 6 slices)	1½ lb liver (about 6 slices)
25 g flour	1 oz flour
Stuffing:	Stuffing:
2 × 15 ml spoons breadcrumbs	2 tablespoons breadcrumbs
1 × 5 ml finely chopped parsley	1 teaspoon finely chopped parsley
½ teaspoon salt	½ teaspoon salt
¼ teaspoon freshly ground black pepper	¼ teaspoon freshly ground black pepper
1 onion, peeled and finely chopped	1 onion, peeled and finely chopped
¼ teaspoon grated lemon rind	¼ teaspoon grated lemon rind
175–225 g bacon, rinded	6–8 oz bacon, rinded
300 ml stock	½ pint stock

Cooking Time: 40 minutes
Oven: 190°C, 375°F, Gas Mark 5

Toss the liver in flour. Mix all the ingredients for the stuffing together, moistening with a little stock. Spread over the liver, wrap each slice with bacon, place in a casserole and pour over the stock so that the liver is covered. Bake about 40 minutes or until the liver is tender. Adjust consistency with beurre manié and taste for seasoning before serving.

Lamb's liver with sherry cream sauce

Metric	Imperial
450 g lamb's liver cut into slices	1 lb lamb's liver cut into slices
2 × 15 ml spoons seasoned flour	2 tablespoons seasoned flour
2 large onions, peeled and sliced	2 large onions, peeled and sliced
50 g butter	2 oz butter
2 × 15 ml spoons cooking sherry	2 tablespoons cooking sherry
150 ml stock	¼ pint stock
4 tomatoes, cut into quarters	4 tomatoes, cut into quarters
Salt and freshly ground black pepper	Salt and freshly ground black pepper
2 × 15 ml spoons single cream	2 tablespoons single cream

Cooking Time: 40 minutes
Oven: 180°C, 350°F, Gas Mark 4

Dip the liver in the seasoned flour. Sweat the onion in the melted butter, transfer to a casserole. Add the liver to the frying pan, fry quickly and place in the casserole. Add extra flour to the pan if necessary to absorb excess fat. Add the sherry, stock and tomatoes, and bring to the boil, stirring. Add to liver in casserole, season well, cover and cook for 30 minutes. Stir in cream and serve with creamed potatoes or rice.

Lamb's liver with sherry cream sauce; Stuffed liver casserole

Today we have an excellent supply of chickens, turkeys and ducks throughout the year because of modern methods of production and deep freezing. All poultry can be used in casseroles and it is an excellent way of giving flavour to frozen, battery bred birds. However all frozen poultry should be thawed before cooking.
The carcase is an added bonus as excellent stock can be made from giblets and bones so that nothing is wasted.
To make stock. Place the carcase and giblets in a saucepan with 1½ l (2½ pints) water, 2 onions, peeled and sliced, 2 carrots, peeled and sliced, 2 sticks of celery washed and sliced, bouquet garni, ¼ teaspoon salt, 12 peppercorns and bring to the boil. Simmer for 1 hour.
Stock can be made in a pressure cooker by following manufacturer's directions.

American chicken casserole

Metric

1 × 15 ml spoon oil
4 chicken drumsticks
2 onions, peeled and sliced
25 g butter
¼ level teaspoon chilli powder
1 × 15 ml spoon flour
150 ml chicken stock
396 g can tomatoes
396 g can kidney beans, drained
Salt and freshly ground black pepper

Imperial

1 tablespoon oil
4 chicken drumsticks
2 onions, peeled and sliced
1 oz butter
¼ level teaspoon chilli powder
1 tablespoon flour
¼ pint chicken stock
14 oz can tomatoes
14 oz can kidney beans, drained
Salt and freshly ground black pepper

Cooking Time: 55 minutes
Oven: 180°C, 350°F, Gas Mark 4

Heat the oil in a frying pan, season the chicken and fry until golden brown. Transfer to a casserole. Fry the onions in the butter, then stir in the chilli powder and flour. Slowly add the stock and bring to the boil. Add the tomatoes and the beans, season well and bring to the boil. Pour over the chicken in the casserole, cover and put in the oven to cook for 45 minutes.

Chicken and peanuts

Metric

5 × 15 ml spoons oil
1 onion, peeled and diced
Salt and freshly ground black pepper
2 × 15 ml spoons flour
4 chicken joints
150 ml stock
150 ml milk
1 × 15 ml spoon peanut butter
2 × 15 ml spoons single cream

To garnish:
50 g salted peanuts

Imperial

5 tablespoons oil
1 onion, peeled and diced
Salt and freshly ground black pepper
2 tablespoons flour
4 chicken joints
¼ pint stock
¼ pint milk
1 tablespoon peanut butter
2 tablespoons single cream

To garnish:
2 oz salted peanuts

Cooking Time: 1¼ hours
Oven: 180°C, 350°F, Gas Mark 4

Heat the oil, sweat the onions for a few minutes and transfer to a casserole. Season the flour and coat chicken well, fry until golden brown and transfer to casserole. Add the stock to the frying pan, stir well and scrape off juices, add milk and peanut butter and heat. Pour over chicken and onions. Cover and cook for 1 hour. Taste and adjust seasoning, add cream and coat each piece of chicken with sauce and garnish with peanuts.

Chicken paella

Chicken paella

Metric

4 × 15 ml spoons oil
2 onions, peeled and sliced
1 green pepper, seeded and sliced
4 tomatoes, peeled and sliced
1 clove garlic, crushed
4 chicken drumsticks
Salt and freshly ground black pepper
225 g rice
¼ teaspoon saffron or turmeric
1 small can crabmeat
100 g prawns
50 g frozen peas
Mussels (optional)
2 × 15 ml spoons white wine (optional)

To garnish:
Finely chopped parsley

Imperial

4 tablespoons oil
2 onions, peeled and sliced
1 green pepper, seeded and sliced
4 tomatoes, peeled and sliced
1 clove garlic, crushed
4 chicken drumsticks
Salt and freshly ground black pepper
8 oz rice
¼ teaspoon saffron or turmeric
1 small can crabmeat
4 oz prawns
2 oz frozen peas
Mussels (optional)
2 tablespoons white wine (optional)

To garnish:
Finely chopped parsley

Cooking Time: 1¼ hours
Oven: 180°C, 350°F, Gas Mark 4

Heat the oil in a frying pan and add the onions, peppers, tomatoes and garlic. Transfer to a casserole and then brown the chicken pieces, add to casserole, season well and cook, covered, for 30 minutes. Meanwhile cook the rice with the saffron in boiling salted water, do not cook through but remove after about 10 minutes, drain. Remove chicken and keep hot. Mix rice with vegetables in casserole, add crabmeat and prawns and peas, replace chicken, season well and cook for a further 40 minutes, covered. Taste and adjust the seasoning. If using mussels wash well and remove the beards, cook over a high heat in wine to open shells. Always discard mussels which do not open. Cover and cook for 20 minutes. Serve with mussels surrounding rice and chicken. Sprinkle with chopped parsley.

Rich chicken casserole

Rich chicken casserole

Metric

4 portions of chicken
2 × 15 ml spoons oil
2 large onions, peeled and
sliced
1 medium-sized carrot,
peeled and diced
2 rashers streaky bacon,
rinded and diced
Salt and freshly ground
black pepper
6 × 15 ml spoons red
wine
300–450 ml stock
Bouquet garni
1 bay leaf
6 small onions, peeled
4 mushrooms, peeled and
sliced
25 g butter
2 × 15 ml spoons flour
2 × 15 ml spoons cream

Imperial

4 portions of chicken
2 tablespoons oil
2 large onions, peeled and
sliced
1 medium-sized carrot,
peeled and diced
2 rashers streaky bacon,
rinded and diced
Salt and freshly ground
black pepper
6 tablespoons red
wine
½–¾ pint stock
Bouquet garni
1 bay leaf
6 small onions, peeled
4 mushrooms, peeled and
sliced
1 oz butter
2 tablespoons flour
2 tablespoons cream

Cooking Time : 1 hour
Oven : 160°C, 325°F, Gas Mark 3

Fry the chicken in oil until golden to seal in the juices, place in the bottom of a casserole. Fry the sliced onions, carrot and bacon, then add to the casserole. Season. Add 4 × 15 ml spoons (4 tablespoons) red wine, stock and herbs. Cover and cook in the oven for 1 hour. Simmer the whole onions in the remaining wine, until tender. Sauté the mushrooms in butter. Remove both and keep warm. Melt the butter, add the flour and cook for a few minutes. Blend in the wine from the onions, together with some stock from the casserole, to make a smooth liquid consistency. Add to the casserole, adjust seasoning. Add onions and mushrooms 15 minutes before serving. Taste and adjust the seasoning. Remove bouquet garni and bay leaf. Stir in the cream at the last minute. Garnish with parsley if liked.

Farmhouse chicken

Metric

1½ kg chicken (oven
ready)
40 g butter
2 sticks celery, washed
and sliced
6 small onions, peeled and
sliced
2 carrots, peeled and
sliced
1 small turnip, peeled
and sliced
300 ml stock
Salt and freshly ground
black pepper

Imperial

3 lb chicken (oven ready)
1½ oz butter
2 sticks celery, washed
and sliced
6 small onions, peeled and
sliced
2 carrots, peeled and
sliced
1 small turnip, peeled and
sliced
½ pint stock
Salt and freshly ground
black pepper

Cooking Time: 1½ hours
Oven: 190°C, 375°F, Gas Mark 5

Melt the butter in a casserole and fry the chicken lightly on
all sides. Add the sliced vegetables, stock and seasoning.
Cover with a lid or foil. Cook about 1½ hours until tender,
baste occasionally with the stock. Taste and adjust the
seasoning. Thicken gravy if necessary.

Braised chicken with peaches

Metric

2 × 15 ml spoons oil
1 × 2 kg chicken
Salt and freshly ground
black pepper
25 g butter
2 onions, peeled and sliced
2 carrots, peeled and
sliced
50 g bacon rashers,
rinded and cut into pieces
¼ teaspoon thyme
1 bay leaf
300 ml peach juice
2 × 5 ml spoons
cornflour
8 peach halves

To garnish:
4 parsley sprigs

Imperial

2 tablespoons oil
1 × 4½ lb chicken
Salt and freshly ground
black pepper
1 oz butter
2 onions, peeled and
sliced
2 carrots, peeled and
sliced
2 oz bacon rashers,
rinded and cut into pieces
¼ teaspoon thyme
1 bay leaf
½ pint peach juice
2 teaspoons cornflour
8 peach halves

To garnish:
4 parsley sprigs

Cooking Time: 1½ hours
Oven: 180°C, 350°F, Gas Mark 4

Heat the oil and brown the chicken. Season well and insert
butter into body, transfer to a casserole. Sweat the onions
and carrots in the oil left from the chicken and add bacon,
put into the casserole. Add thyme, bay leaf and peach juice,
season well, cover and cook. Taste and adjust the seasoning.
Carve on to a serving plate surrounded by halved peaches,
return to oven to heat. Remove fat by skimming. Thicken
sauce, strain and pour over or serve separately. Garnish
with sprigs of parsley.

Chicken with walnuts

Metric

4 chicken joints
50 g butter
1 leek, washed and sliced
4 button onions, peeled
450 ml chicken stock
1 sprig thyme
2 × 15 ml spoons wine
vinegar
Salt and freshly ground
black pepper
50 g walnuts, chopped

To garnish:
Finely chopped parsley
Walnut halves
1 × 15 ml spoon cream
(optional)

Imperial

4 chicken joints
2 oz butter
1 leek, washed and sliced
4 button onions, peeled
¾ pint chicken stock
1 sprig thyme
2 tablespoons wine
vinegar
Salt and freshly ground
black pepper
2 oz walnuts, chopped

To garnish:
Finely chopped parsley
Walnut halves
1 tablespoon cream
(optional)

Cooking Time: 50 minutes
Oven: 180°C, 350°F, Gas Mark 4

Fry the chicken joints in the butter until golden brown,
drain and place in a casserole. Toss the sliced leek and
whole onions in the butter. Place the vegetables, stock,
thyme and wine vinegar over the chicken. Season well.
Cover and cook for 30 minutes. Remove the joints and keep
hot. Liquidise the walnuts with the onion mixture and some
of the liquid. Pour over the chicken in the casserole and
cook for 15 minutes. Taste and adjust the seasoning. Garnish with parsley and walnut halves and dribble with cream.

Farmhouse chicken; Chicken with walnuts; Braised chicken with peaches

Casseroled turkey with red wine

Metric

3–4 kg small turkey
½ teaspoon allspice
Finely grated rind of
1 lemon
50 g butter
8 small onions, peeled
Salt and freshly ground
black pepper
1 bay leaf
1 sprig or ¼ teaspoon
thyme
Parsley sprig
300 ml red wine
225 g button mushrooms,
washed
150 ml cranberries,
sieved

Imperial

7–8 lb small turkey
½ teaspoon allspice
Finely grated rind of
1 lemon
2 oz butter
8 small onions, peeled
Salt and freshly ground
black pepper
1 bay leaf
1 sprig or ¼ teaspoon
thyme
Parsley sprig
½ pint red wine
8 oz button mushrooms,
washed
¼ pint cranberries, sieved

Cooking Time: 2½ hours approx.
Oven: 200°C, 400°F, Gas Mark 6
    160°C, 325°F, Gas Mark 3

Remove giblet bag, if inside, from turkey and make the contents into stock with a little water. Sprinkle the inside of the bird with allspice, lemon rind and about 15 g (½ oz) butter. Rub remaining butter all over the turkey and season well. Place the turkey on its side to brown in a hot oven, with onions. Turn over after 15 minutes. Transfer bird and onions when brown into a casserole or, if you do not have one which is large enough, use the roasting tin covered with foil. Reduce heat to 160°C, 325°F, Gas Mark 3. Take 1 pint of giblet stock, add herbs and wine, heat and pour over the bird and onions. Cook in a fairly moderate oven for 1½ hours. Cook the mushrooms for the last 15 minutes with bird. Test for readiness by pricking with a skewer, juice should be clear not pink, to indicate turkey is cooked. Carve onto a heated serving dish. Remove the bay leaf and herbs. Thicken gravy with a beurre manié of flour and butter whisked in, then add sieved or liquidised cranberries to the sauce and pour over the turkey. Serve with a green salad with walnuts.

Chicken mexico

Metric

1½–1¾ kg chicken
40 g butter
2 × 15 ml spoons oil
2 large onions, peeled and
sliced
2 cloves garlic, crushed
1 green pepper, seeded and
sliced
1 chilli pepper
175 g can tomatoes
2 × 15 ml spoons tomato
purée
300 ml chicken stock or
stock and wine
100 g sweet corn
4 × 15 ml spoons soured
cream
100 g mushrooms, washed
and sliced
Finely chopped parsley

Imperial

3–4 lb chicken
1½ oz butter
2 tablespoons oil
2 large onions, peeled and
sliced
2 cloves garlic, crushed
1 green pepper, seeded and
sliced
1 chilli pepper
7 oz can tomatoes
2 tablespoons tomato
purée
½ pint chicken stock or
stock and wine
4 oz sweet corn
4 tablespoons soured
cream
4 oz mushrooms, washed
and sliced
Finely chopped parsley

Cooking Time: 1½ hours
Oven: 160°C, 325°F, Gas Mark 3

Brown the chicken in butter and oil on all sides. Remove from fat and place in a casserole. Fry onions, garlic, pepper and chilli. Add tomatoes, tomato purée and the stock and wine. Pour over the chicken and cook in covered casserole in the oven for 1¼ hours. Allow chicken to cool in the juice, then carve and put on a serving dish and keep hot. Meanwhile heat the corn. Boil up the sauce until reduced by half, add cream and stir. Add mushrooms and cook for a few minutes. Pour over chicken with parsley and sweet corn. Serve with rice.
(Ideal to make the day before and be really organised for your guests. Chicken is really best left overnight in sauce in the refrigerator.)

Duck with cherries; Chicken with grapefruit; Tarragon chicken; Chicken normande

Duck with cherries

Metric

1 duck
300 ml stock
1 onion, peeled
Finely grated rind of
1 lemon
Salt and freshly ground
black pepper
453 g can black cherries
cherries
1 × 15 ml spoon
cornflour

To garnish:
Watercress sprigs

Imperial

1 duck
½ pint stock
1 onion, peeled
Finely grated rind of
1 lemon
Salt and freshly ground
black pepper
16 oz can black cherries
1 tablespoon cornflour

To garnish:
Watercress sprigs

Cooking Time: 1½ hours
Oven: 190°C, 375°F, Gas Mark 5

Place the duck in the casserole with the onion, cover and cook with the stock for 30 minutes. Remove the liquid from the casserole and retain. Sprinkle with grated lemon rind and seasoning. Pour over the cherries, retaining a few for the garnish, and juice. Cover and cook for 1 hour or until the duck is cooked. Skim fat from first cooking liquid and thicken with cornflour. Add to the casserole and cook for a further 5 minutes. The sauce may be served from the casserole or may be sieved or liquidised as desired. Garnish with fresh watercress and whole cherries if available.

Tarragon chicken

Metric

25 g butter
2 rashers streaky bacon, rinded and chopped
2 onions, peeled and sliced
2 carrots, peeled and sliced
4 chicken portions
50 g chicken livers
3 tarragon sprigs
300 ml chicken stock
1 × 15 ml spoon sweet sherry
Salt and freshly ground black pepper
1 × 5 ml spoon cornflour
To garnish:
Tarragon sprigs

Imperial

1 oz butter
2 rashers streaky bacon, rinded and chopped
2 onions, peeled and sliced
2 carrots, peeled and sliced
4 chicken portions
2 oz chicken livers
3 tarragon sprigs
½ pint chicken stock
1 tablespoon sweet sherry
Salt and freshly ground black pepper
1 teaspoon cornflour
To garnish:
Tarragon sprigs

Cooking Time: 1 hour
Oven: 160°C, 325°F, Gas Mark 3

Melt the butter in a frying pan and add the bacon, onions and carrots, cook for a few minutes, transfer to a casserole. Brown the chicken on both sides and transfer to the casserole. Finally brown the chicken livers and place around chicken. Add tarragon, stock, sherry, seasoning, cover and cook. Thicken gravy with cornflour and pour back over chicken. Taste and adjust the seasoning. Garnish with fresh tarragon if available.

Chicken normande

Metric

25 g seedless raisins
50 g butter
4 chicken joints
Salt and freshly ground black pepper
700 g apples, peeled, cored and sliced
2 × 15 ml spoons lemon juice
2 × 15 ml spoons cider
½ teaspoon cinnamon
150 ml double cream

Imperial

1 oz seedless raisins
2 oz butter
4 chicken joints
Salt and freshly ground black pepper
1½ lb apples, peeled, cored and sliced
2 tablespoons lemon juice
2 tablespoons cider
½ teaspoon cinnamon
¼ pint double cream

Cooking Time: 1¼ hours
Oven: 160°C, 325°F, Gas Mark 3

Soak the raisins for 1 hour in warm water. Heat half the butter in a frying pan and brown the chicken pieces on all sides. Remove to a plate and season well. Add remaining butter and toss in the apple slices so that they become lightly browned only. Place half the apples in the bottom of a casserole and arrange chicken on top. Mix together the lemon juice, cider, salt and black pepper, cinnamon and raisins. Add remaining apples round the chicken, season and pour the raisin mixture over the chicken and apples. Cover with a piece of greaseproof paper and a tight-fitting lid, and cook for about 1 hour. Stir in the cream and return to the oven to heat through for 5 minutes. Taste and adjust the seasoning.

Chicken with grapefruit

Metric

25 g butter
4 pieces of chicken
Salt and freshly ground black pepper
2 × 5 ml spoons brandy
300 ml chicken stock
2 × 15 ml spoons sherry
1 × 5 ml spoon dried herbs
1 grapefruit
1 × 15 ml spoon cornflour
2 × 15 ml spoons sugar

To garnish:
Watercress

Imperial

1 oz butter
4 pieces of chicken
Salt and freshly ground black pepper
2 teaspoons brandy
½ pint chicken stock
2 tablespoons sherry
1 teaspoon dried herbs
1 grapefruit
1 tablespoon cornflour
2 tablespoons sugar

To garnish:
Watercress

Cooking Time: 1¼ hours
Oven: 160°C, 325°F, Gas Mark 3

Melt butter in a frying pan and brown chicken on all sides. Remove to a casserole or brown in casserole, season well. Heat brandy in a ladle and set alight, remove chicken from heat and pour over the brandy. Add the stock and sherry and herbs, cover and simmer for 1 hour. Meanwhile remove thin strips of grapefruit peel with a sharp knife. Cut the grapefruit across the top and cut round skin removing all the white pith. Cut into each segment to obtain a slice without skin. Squeeze remaining grapefruit with the hand into the casserole juice. Taste and adjust the seasoning. Thicken stock if necessary with the cornflour adding the sugar and strips of grapefruit peel. Garnish chicken with watercress and grapefruit segments if available.

Boned chicken with apricots

Metric	Imperial
1 × 1½ kg chicken, boned	1 × 3 lb chicken, boned
396 g can apricot halves, drained	14 oz can apricot halves, drained
Salt and freshly ground black pepper	Salt and freshly ground black pepper
50 g butter	2 oz butter
1 × 15 ml spoon finely chopped parsley	1 tablespoon finely chopped parsley
2 onions, peeled and thinly sliced	2 onions, peeled and thinly sliced
1 clove garlic, crushed	1 clove garlic, crushed
150 ml white wine	¼ pint white wine

Cooking Time: 1½ hours
Oven: 180°C, 350°F, Gas Mark 4

This is a special dinner party dish which requires a boned chicken, but is easy to prepare in advance.

Bone the chicken by cutting down the backbone and easing flesh away. Cut round leg joints and push flesh down, removing sinews, remove thigh bone. Keep bird on its front and ease all flesh off until the carcass is released from breast bone. Save some apricot halves for garnish. Stuff pairs of apricot halves with a mixture of 25 g (1 oz) seasoned butter and parsley. Arrange pairs down the centre of the chicken. Season well and sew up to ensure there are no holes. Melt the remaining butter and brown the chicken on all sides, turn down heat, add onions and garlic and cook for a few minutes. Season well, add white wine and apricot juice, cover and cook. Remove string before serving. Serve garnished with the remaining apricots and the golden brown sauce which should be poured over. This is a very easy dish to carve for a dinner party.

Turkey in riesling

Metric	Imperial
25 g butter	1 oz butter
4 turkey legs or portions	4 turkey legs or portions
4 spring onions, washed and chopped	4 spring onions, washed and chopped
100 g mushrooms, washed and sliced	4 oz mushrooms, washed and sliced
Salt and freshly ground black pepper	Salt and freshly ground black pepper
150 ml riesling wine	¼ pint riesling wine
4 × 15 ml spoons double cream	4 tablespoons double cream
To garnish:	To garnish:
Finely chopped parsley	Finely chopped parsley

Cooking Time: 1¼ hours
Oven: 160°C, 350°F, Gas Mark 4

Heat the butter in a frying pan and brown the turkey on all sides, lower heat and add spring onions and sliced mushrooms. Transfer to a casserole, season well. Add wine, cover and cook for ¾ hour, add cream and cook for a further 15 minutes. Taste and adjust the seasoning. Serve sprinkled with chopped parsley.

Braised turkey with mushrooms

Metric	Imperial
25 g butter	1 oz butter
1 onion, peeled and sliced	1 onion, peeled and sliced
1 clove garlic, peeled and crushed	1 clove garlic, peeled and crushed
1 × 1 kg rolled turkey breast	1 × 2 lb rolled turkey breast
¼ teaspoon nutmeg	¼ teaspoon nutmeg
Salt and freshly ground black pepper	Salt and freshly ground black pepper
225 g mushrooms, washed and sliced	8 oz mushrooms, washed and sliced
300 ml chicken stock	½ pint chicken stock
Bouquet garni	Bouquet garni
To garnish:	To garnish:
Finely chopped parsley	Finely chopped parsley

Cooking Time: 1 hour
Oven: 180°C, 350°F, Gas Mark 4

Melt the butter in a casserole and sweat onions and garlic for a few minutes. Add rolled turkey breast, sprinkle with nutmeg and seasoning. Add mushrooms, pour on the stock, add bouquet garni. Cover and cook. Remove the bouquet garni. Carve and serve breast slices covered with mushrooms on a heated plate. Reduce stock and thicken with 15 g (½ oz) beurre manié, if liked. Garnish with chopped parsley if liked.

Turkey in riesling; Boned chicken with apricots; Braised turkey with mushrooms

This is a term which applies to animals and birds which are hunted at certain times of the year and protected during breeding times. Pigeons, rabbits, hare and venison are available most of the year and are excellent in casseroles. Pheasants, grouse and partridge are also excellent cooked in a casserole as they can be dry when roasted unless cooked very carefully. It is now possible to buy game ready prepared and frozen in supermarkets and it is well worth experimenting to add variety to the menu.

Pheasant with mushrooms and onions

Metric

2 × 15 ml spoons oil
25 g butter
2 large onions, peeled and thinly sliced
3 carrots, peeled and thinly sliced
¼ teaspoon thyme
¼ teaspoon chervil
¼ teaspoon rosemary
¼ teaspoon parsley
2 bay leaves
1 pheasant
300 ml water
300 ml red wine
1 × 15 ml spoon brandy
Salt and freshly ground black pepper
25 g butter
8 small onions, peeled
8 whole mushrooms, washed

Beurre manié
25 g butter with
25 g flour
2 × 15 ml spoons cream

To garnish:
Watercress

Imperial

2 tablespoons oil
1 oz butter
2 large onions, peeled and thinly sliced
3 carrots, peeled and thinly sliced
¼ teaspoon thyme
¼ teaspoon chervil
¼ teaspoon rosemary
¼ teaspoon parsley
2 bay leaves
1 pheasant
½ pint water
½ pint red wine
1 tablespoon brandy
Salt and freshly ground black pepper
1 oz butter
8 small onions, peeled
8 whole mushrooms, washed

Beurre manié
1 oz butter with
1 oz flour
2 tablespoons cream

To garnish:
Watercress

Cooking Time: 1½ hours
Oven: 160°C, 325°F, Gas Mark 3

Cut the pheasant into 4 serving portions with poultry shears or the butcher will do this for you. Heat the oil and butter in a frying pan. Add the onions and carrots and cook over a gentle heat for 5 minutes. Add herbs, stir well and transfer to a casserole. Sauté the pheasant in the remaining fat on a fairly high heat, turning round to brown evenly. Remove the bird to casserole. Add water to the frying pan with half the wine and heat so that all sediment is removed from frying pan. Heat brandy in a ladle, set alight and pour over the pheasant. When the flames have died away, pour over the wine mixture from the frying pan and season. Place in the oven uncovered for 1 hour, basting with juice from time to time. Meanwhile melt the butter in the frying pan, add the small onions and cook for 5–7 minutes over a low heat, but do not allow to become too brown. Add mushrooms and remaining wine, stir round in the pan and cover. Allow to cook gently for 10 minutes until wine is reduced to a glaze. Remove bay leaves. Remove the pheasant to a serving dish and keep warm. Reduce the liquid by half and thicken with the beurre manié. Add the onions and mushrooms and cook gently for 2–3 minutes. Taste and adjust the seasoning. Finally stir in cream and pour over pheasant. Garnish with watercress.
Cock birds are larger than hen birds and will serve 4. Use 2 hen pheasants for 6 servings.

Pheasant with mushrooms and onions

Pheasant casserole in red wine

Pheasant casserole in red wine

Metric	Imperial
1 pheasant	*1 pheasant*
15 g butter	*½ oz butter*
1 × 15 ml spoon oil	*1 tablespoon oil*
2 onions, finely chopped	*2 onions, finely chopped*
1 clove garlic, peeled and crushed	*1 clove garlic, peeled and crushed*
1 carrot, peeled and diced	*1 carrot, peeled and diced*
2 sticks celery, washed and sliced	*2 sticks celery, washed and sliced*
Pinch marjoram and thyme	*Pinch marjoram and thyme*
1 bay leaf	*1 bay leaf*
Salt and freshly ground black pepper	*Salt and freshly ground black pepper*
150 ml red wine	*¼ pint red wine*
150 ml stock or water	*¼ pint stock or water*

Beurre manié
15 g butter with
15 g flour

Beurre manié
½ oz butter with
½ oz flour

Cooking Time: 1¼ hours
Oven: 180°C, 350°F, Gas Mark 4

Brown whole pheasant in butter and oil, transfer to casserole. Place vegetables in frying pan and sauté gently for 5 minutes. Turn into the casserole. Add herbs, seasoning, wine and stock to frying pan, scrape down pan juices and pour into casserole. Cover and cook for 1 hour until tender. Remove pheasant to a clean casserole or dish and keep warm. Skim fat from the sauce, remove bay leaf and reduce by half, then thicken by whisking in beurre manié. Taste and adjust the seasoning. Pour over the pheasant.

Pigeon casserole

Pigeon casserole

Metric

4 rashers fat bacon,
rinded and diced
25 g butter
4 small pigeons, plucked
and cleaned
2 small onions, peeled and
sliced
1 carrot, peeled and sliced
100 g mushrooms, washed
and sliced
50 g flour
600 ml stock
Salt and freshly ground
black pepper

Forcemeat balls:
(optional)
100 g fresh breadcrumbs
50 g suet
1 × 15 ml spoon finely
chopped parsley
Grated rind ½ lemon
Salt and freshly ground
black pepper
Beaten egg to bind

Imperial

4 rashers fat bacon,
rinded and diced
1 oz butter
4 small pigeons, plucked
and cleaned
2 small onions, peeled and
sliced
1 carrot, peeled and
sliced
4 oz mushrooms, washed
and sliced
2 oz flour
1 pint stock
Salt and freshly ground
black pepper

Forcemeat balls:
(optional)
4 oz fresh breadcrumbs
2 oz suet
1 tablespoon finely
chopped parsley
Grated rind ½ lemon
Salt and freshly ground
black pepper
Beaten egg to bind

Cooking Time: 1¼ hours
Oven: 180°C, 350°F, Gas Mark 4

Fry the bacon in heated butter until brown, remove to a casserole. Remove the feet from pigeons, fry until brown, place in the casserole. Fry the onions, carrot and mushrooms lightly, drain and remove to the casserole. Stir in flour to frying pan, heat gently until brown, stirring all the time. Add the stock, season to taste and bring to the boil and pour into casserole. Cover and cook in the oven until tender. Mix up ingredients for forcemeat and form into small balls, add to the casserole and cook for a further 15 minutes.

Serve garnished with triangles of toast or fried bread, if liked, and chopped parsley.

Rabbit casserole

Metric

1 rabbit, cut into joints
1 × 15 ml spoon flour
Salt and freshly ground
black pepper
50 g streaky bacon,
rinded and chopped
25 g butter
1 × 15 ml spoon oil
12 small onions, peeled
2 sticks celery, washed
and sliced
1 red pepper, seeded
and cut into strips
4 × 15 ml spoons white
wine
150 ml chicken stock
2 rosemary sprigs or
½ teaspoon dried
rosemary

Beurre manié
15 g butter with
15 g flour

Imperial

1 rabbit, cut into joints
1 tablespoon flour
Salt and freshly ground
black pepper
2 oz streaky bacon,
rinded and chopped
1 oz butter
1 tablespoon oil
12 small onions, peeled
2 sticks celery, washed
and sliced
1 red pepper, seeded
and cut into strips
4 tablespoons white wine
¼ pint chicken stock
2 rosemary sprigs or
½ teaspoon dried
rosemary

Beurre manié
½ oz butter with
½ oz flour

Cooking Time: 1 hour
Oven: 150°C, 300°F, Gas Mark 2

Prepare the rabbit and dip in seasoned flour. Place the bacon in the butter and oil and sauté gently. Remove to a casserole. Place the joints in the fat and brown on all sides. Transfer to the casserole. Sauté the onions gently, then add to the bacon. Sauté the celery and pepper gently, then add to the casserole. Pour over the wine, stock, rosemary and seasoning. Cover and cook gently for at least 1 hour. Serve the joints on a heated serving dish with the whole onions. Thicken the sauce with the beurre manié and whisk well until smooth. Pour over the rabbit and serve.

Rabbit casserole

Jugged hare

Metric

1 hare with blood
4 rashers streaky bacon, rinded
25 g butter
2 onions, peeled and finely diced
2 carrots, peeled and finely diced
2 sticks celery, washed and thinly sliced
1 bay leaf
1 sprig parsley or
$\frac{1}{4} \times 5$ ml spoon dried
1 thyme sprig or
$\frac{1}{4}$ teaspoon dried
Salt and freshly ground black pepper
1 l stock
2 × 15 ml spoons redcurrant jelly
4 × 15 ml spoons port

Imperial

1 hare with blood
4 rashers streaky bacon, rinded
1 oz butter
2 onions, peeled and finely diced
2 carrots, peeled and finely diced
2 sticks celery, washed and thinly sliced
1 bay leaf
1 sprig parsley or
$\frac{1}{4}$ teaspoon dried
1 thyme sprig or
$\frac{1}{4}$ teaspoon dried
Salt and freshly ground black pepper
$1\frac{3}{4}$ pints stock
2 tablespoons redcurrant jelly
4 tablespoons port

Cooking Time: $3\frac{1}{2}$ hours
Oven: 160°C, 325°F, Gas Mark 3

Joint the hare or ask the butcher to do it for you. Retain the blood. Gently fry streaky bacon in a frying pan until the fat runs out. Remove bacon to a casserole and fry joints of hare until golden brown, remove to the casserole. Add butter to the frying pan and cook the diced vegetables gently for about 3–4 minutes. Add the vegetables to the hare in the casserole with the herbs and season well. Boil up the stock in the frying pan and pour into the casserole, cover and cook in the oven for $2\frac{1}{2}$–3 hours, until hare is tender. Strain the gravy from the casserole, remove hare on to a heated dish. Return juice to the casserole, add the redcurrant jelly and port, bring to just under boiling point, simmer for a few minutes, taste and adjust the seasoning. Remove from the heat, gradually stir in the blood and reheat without allowing to boil. Strain the sauce over the hare.

Jugged hare

It is usual to cook vegetables quickly to avoid loss of nutrients but many vegetables are excellent in casserole dishes and can even be cooked as a main meal to add variety to our menu planning. Firm vegetables such as peppers, celery, marrows, courgettes are often blanched by placing in boiling water for a few minutes before being used in the casserole dish. Stuffed peppers, aubergines and marrows are all excellent additions to the casserole range, whether stuffed with rice, chicken or meat.

Country vegetable casserole; Potato and tomato casserole; Cabbage and celery casserole

Potato and tomato casserole

Metric

25 g butter
2 large onions, peeled and thinly sliced
1 clove garlic, crushed (optional)
450 g potatoes, peeled and thinly sliced
Salt and freshly ground black pepper
300 ml stock

Topping:
2 tomatoes, thinly sliced
50 g cheese, grated
1 × 5 ml spoon chopped chives

Imperial

1 oz butter
2 large onions, peeled and thinly sliced
1 clove garlic, crushed (optional)
1 lb potatoes, peeled and thinly sliced
Salt and freshly ground black pepper
½ pint stock

Topping:
2 tomatoes, thinly sliced
2 oz cheese, grated
1 teaspoon chopped chives

Cooking Time: 1¼ hours
Oven: 160°C, 325°F, Gas Mark 3

Melt the butter in a frying pan and gently sauté the sliced onion and crushed garlic. Place a layer of onion and garlic alternately in a casserole with thinly sliced potatoes, seasoning well between each layer. Pour over the hot stock and cover the casserole. Put into the oven and cook until the vegetables are tender and the stock is absorbed. Top with sliced tomatoes and grated cheese. Brown under the grill before serving and sprinkle with chopped chives. Cut into portions to serve with chops, steak or beefburgers although it is delicious on its own.

Country vegetable casserole

Metric

50 g butter
2 large onions, thinly sliced
4 new carrots, thinly sliced
1 new turnip, thinly sliced
1 leek, sliced
2 potatoes, thinly sliced
250 g pkt frozen corn and sweet peppers
Salt and freshly ground black pepper
300 ml stock
50 g cheese, grated

Imperial

2 oz butter
2 large onions, thinly sliced
4 new carrots, thinly sliced
1 new turnip, thinly sliced
1 leek, sliced
2 potatoes, thinly sliced
8 oz pkt frozen corn and sweet peppers
Salt and freshly ground black pepper
½ pint stock
2 oz cheese, grated

Cooking Time: 1 hour
Oven: 180°C, 350°F, Gas Mark 4

Melt the butter in an ovenproof casserole. Toss in the sliced onions and leave on a low heat for about 5 minutes. Add the thinly sliced vegetables and the corn and sweet peppers, with seasoning between each layer. Pour over the stock, cover the casserole and cook in the oven for 45 minutes or until the vegetables have absorbed the stock. Sprinkle with the grated cheese and brown under the grill.

Cabbage and celery casserole

Metric

50 g butter
1 small onion, peeled and sliced
1 small head celery, washed and sliced
½ small white cabbage, washed and shredded
25 g butter
25 g flour
300 ml milk
Salt and freshly ground black pepper
25 g fresh white breadcrumbs
25 g butter

Imperial

2 oz butter
1 small onion, peeled and sliced
1 small head celery, washed and sliced
½ small white cabbage, washed and shredded
1 oz butter
1 oz flour
½ pint milk
Salt and freshly ground black pepper
1 oz fresh white breadcrumbs
1 oz butter

Cooking Time: 30 minutes
Oven: 180°C, 350°F, Gas Mark 4

Melt the butter in a frying pan, add the onion and celery and cook gently for 5 minutes, stirring from time to time. Add the cabbage and allow to simmer on a gentle heat for a further 5 minutes. Melt the butter in a saucepan and add the flour to make a roux. Add the milk gradually, stirring with a wooden spoon until a smooth sauce is formed. Season well. Turn the vegetables into a 1 l (2 pint) casserole and season well. Pour the sauce over the vegetables and sprinkle with breadcrumbs dotted with butter. Cover and cook in the oven for 20 minutes until the crumb topping is golden brown.

Stuffed cabbage leaves

Metric	Imperial
8 large cabbage leaves	8 large cabbage leaves
100 g cooked rice	4 oz cooked rice
100 g cooked chicken meat	4 oz cooked chicken meat
1 × 15 ml spoon sweet corn and pepper mixture	1 tablespoon sweetcorn and pepper mixture
1 small onion, finely diced	1 small onion, finely diced
Few drops Tabasco sauce	Few drops Tabasco sauce
Salt and freshly ground black pepper	Salt and freshly ground black pepper

Metric	Imperial
Tomato sauce:	Tomato sauce:
1 × 15 ml spoon oil	1 tablespoon oil
1 onion, finely diced	1 onion, finely diced
396 g can of tomatoes	14 oz can tomatoes
150 ml chicken stock	¼ pint chicken stock
2 × 5 ml spoons oregano	2 teaspoons oregano
Few drops Tabasco sauce	Few drops Tabasco sauce
1 × 15 ml spoon tomato purée	1 tablespoon tomato purée
1 × 5 ml spoon lemon juice	1 teaspoon lemon juice
Salt and freshly ground black pepper	Salt and freshly ground black pepper

Cooking Time: 35 minutes
Oven: 180°C, 350°F, Gas Mark 4

Blanch cabbage leaves. Mix all other ingredients well and spoon out into portions on to cabbage leaves. Tie the leaves up into 'parcels' with fine string or fasten with cocktail sticks. Place in casserole dish.

To make the tomato sauce, sauté the onion in the oil for 4–5 minutes. Add all other ingredients and bring to the boil. Taste and adjust the seasoning. Now pour the sauce mixture through a sieve over the stuffed cabbage leaves, cover and cook in the oven for 25 minutes.

Artichokes au gratin

Metric	Imperial
450 g Jerusalem artichokes	1 lb Jerusalem artichokes
300 ml milk	½ pint milk
300 ml water	½ pint water
½ teaspoon salt	½ teaspoon salt
100 g mushrooms, washed and chopped	4 oz mushrooms, washed and chopped
1 onion, peeled and diced	1 onion, peeled and diced
25 g butter	1 oz butter
25 g flour	1 oz flour
Salt and freshly ground black pepper	Salt and freshly ground black pepper
2 × 15 ml spoons single cream	2 tablespoons single cream
25 g fresh breadcrumbs	1 oz fresh breadcrumbs
25 g cheese, grated	1 oz cheese, grated

Cooking Time: 40 minutes
Oven: 180°C, 350°F, Gas Mark 4

Peel the artichokes and place in a saucepan with the milk, water and salt. Bring to the boil slowly and simmer for 10 minutes or until tender. Arrange in a casserole, cover with the mushrooms and onions. Melt the butter in a saucepan, add flour to make a roux, then pour in 450 ml (¾ pint) of the artichoke liquid, stir well until you have a thin sauce, season well. Pour into the casserole and cook in the oven, covered, for 15 minutes. Remove the lid, sprinkle with the cream, breadcrumbs and grated cheese, return to the oven for a further 15 minutes.

Mushrooms à la grecque

Metric	Imperial
225 g mushrooms, washed and sliced	8 oz mushrooms, washed and sliced
1 onion, peeled and sliced	1 onion, peeled and sliced
2 × 15 ml spoons olive oil	2 tablespoons olive oil
1 × 15 ml spoon tomato purée	1 tablespoon tomato purée
2 bay leaves	2 bay leaves
6 peppercorns	6 peppercorns
150 ml chicken stock	¼ pint chicken stock
2 × 15 ml spoons dry white wine	2 tablespoons dry white wine
Salt and freshly ground black pepper	Salt and freshly ground black pepper

Cooking Time: 30–40 minutes
Oven: 160°C, 325°F, Gas Mark 3

Slice the mushrooms through the stems and blanch for 2 minutes. Sauté the onion in the oil. Arrange the mushrooms in a casserole and add the remaining ingredients. Cover and cook in the oven for 30–40 minutes. Remove bay leaves and peppercorns. Serve sprinkled with paprika and chopped parsley.

Stuffed cabbage leaves; Mushrooms à la grecque; Artichokes au gratin

Fish has fairly tender flesh and it is therefore unnecessary to give it long, slow cooking in most cases but whole fish and thick steaks can be casseroled for ease of cooking.
Fish stock can be made from heads, tails, bones, placed in water, (1 kg (2 lb) fish pieces – 2 l (3½ pints) water), 2 onions, peeled and sliced, 1 carrot, peeled and sliced, 1 stick of celery, washed and sliced, 150 ml (¼ pint) dry white wine, ¼ teaspoon salt, 12 peppercorns and a bouquet garni.
Most fish may be poached in the oven in fish stock, in a casserole and a sauce made from the liquid to accompany the fish.

Fish with grapes

Metric

175 g green grapes, halved and seeded
450 g flaked white fish, cooked in milk
2 × 15 ml spoons fresh cream
Salt and freshly ground black pepper
450 g mashed potato
1 beaten egg
2 × 15 ml spoons milk
100 g cheese, grated
25 g butter

To garnish:
Green grapes, halved and seeded

Imperial

6 oz green grapes, halved and seeded
1 lb flaked white fish, cooked in milk
2 tablespoons fresh cream
Salt and freshly ground black pepper
1 lb mashed potato
1 beaten egg
2 tablespoons milk
4 oz cheese, grated
1 oz butter

To garnish:
Green grapes, halved and seeded

Cooking Time: 20 minutes
Oven: 180°C, 350°F, Gas Mark 4

Butter a casserole. Arrange seeded grapes over the bottom of dish. Mix fish with milk, cream and seasoning and place over grapes. Mix potato with the egg and milk, season and place over the fish. Score the top with a fork. Cover and bake for 20 minutes. Remove cover. Sprinkle with cheese and dot with the butter and grill until brown. Garnish with green grapes.

Salmon with hollandaise sauce

Metric

1 × 2 kg salmon trout, or 4 thick salmon steaks
Salt and freshly ground black pepper
Fish stock (see above)
2 × 15 ml spoons white wine

Hollandaise sauce:
3 × 15 ml spoons wine vinegar
6 peppercorns, slightly crushed
Bay leaf
Blade of mace
2 egg yolks
100 g butter

To garnish:
Asparagus spears (optional)
Hard-boiled egg (optional)

Imperial

1 × 4 lb salmon trout, or 4 thick salmon steaks
Salt and freshly ground black pepper
Fish stock (see above)
2 tablespoons white wine

Hollandaise sauce:
3 tablespoons wine vinegar
6 peppercorns, slightly crushed
Bay leaf
Blade of mace
2 egg yolks
4 oz butter

To garnish:
Asparagus spears (optional)
Hard-boiled egg (optional)

Cooking Time: 30 minutes
Oven: 160°C, 325°F, Gas Mark 3

Clean the salmon trout making sure all the blood is removed from the backbone and wash under the cold tap. Do not remove scales as they give protection. Place in a casserole, season and pour the court bouillon on to the fish with a little extra white wine if desired. (A large salmon which is too big for a casserole may be cooked between two large roasting tins if you do not have a fish kettle). If using steaks place in the casserole and cover with the court bouillon in the same way. Cover and cook in the oven. Serve hot garnished with asparagus or hard-boiled egg and Hollandaise sauce.
To make the sauce: Put the vinegar, slightly crushed peppercorns, bay leaf and mace in a saucepan and reduce over a medium heat until only 1 × 15 ml spoon (1 tablespoon) remains. Place the egg yolks in a bowl with a knob of butter and beat together. Add the liquid and place bowl over a saucepan of hot water. Stir all the time and gradually add remaining softened butter, a little at a time until it is all added. A rich buttery sauce results, adjust seasoning. A few drops of lemon juice can be added if sauce is too thick. Do not leave the sauce over hot water or it will begin to set after it is cooked.

Sole with prawns; Smoked haddock and bacon casserole; Haddock flamenco

Haddock flamenco

Metric

¾ kg haddock fillet,
skinned
Salt and freshly ground
black pepper
225 g courgettes, washed
and sliced
1 medium-sized onion,
peeled and sliced
25 g butter
2 medium-sized tomatoes,
skinned and chopped
¼ teaspoon Tabasco
sauce

Imperial

1¼ lb haddock fillet,
skinned
Salt and freshly ground
black pepper
8 oz courgettes, washed
and sliced
1 medium-sized onion,
peeled and sliced
1 oz butter
2 medium-sized tomatoes,
skinned and chopped
¼ teaspoon Tabasco
sauce

Cooking Time: 30 minutes
Oven: 200°C, 400°F, Gas Mark 6

Cut haddock into 4 equal portions, and season each piece
with salt and pepper. Fry courgettes and onion in butter
until just tender, then stir in tomatoes and Tabasco sauce.
Place portions of haddock in a casserole, then top fish with
vegetables. Cover and cook in the oven until haddock and
vegetables are tender.

Smoked haddock and bacon casserole

Metric

4 smoked haddock cutlets
25 g butter
Freshly ground black
pepper
4 rashers back bacon,
rinded
150 ml milk

To garnish:
Slices of bread, toasted
Chopped parsley

Imperial

4 smoked haddock cutlets
1 oz butter
Freshly ground black
pepper
4 rashers back bacon,
rinded
¼ pint milk

To garnish:
Slices of bread, toasted
Chopped parsley

Cooking Time: 25 minutes
Oven: 160°C, 325°F, Gas Mark 3

Remove the tail from the haddock and arrange in a casserole rubbed over with a quarter of the butter. Season fish well with pepper and divide remaining butter between fish and dot on top. Lay a rasher of bacon on each fish. Pour in the milk and cook in the oven, covered. Make the toast and cut into triangles. Serve with the fish, garnished with chopped parsley. With a poached egg this dish makes an excellent brunch or high tea.

Sole with prawns

Metric

4 sole or plaice, filleted
100 g peeled prawns
Salt and freshly ground
black pepper
300 ml fish stock
6 peppercorns
Blade of mace
2 × 5 ml spoons lemon
juice
25 g butter
25 g flour
2 × 15 ml spoons single
cream (optional)

To garnish:
Parsley sprigs

Imperial

4 sole or plaice, filleted
4 oz peeled prawns
Salt and freshly ground
black pepper
½ pint fish stock
6 peppercorns
Blade of mace
2 teaspoons lemon juice
1 oz butter
1 oz flour
2 tablespoons single cream
(optional)

To garnish:
Parsley sprigs

Cooking Time: 25 minutes
Oven: 160°C, 325°F, Gas Mark 3

Wash and dry the fish. Divide half the prawns between the fish fillets, season to taste, roll up and place in a buttered ovenproof casserole. Cover with the fish stock, made by simmering the fish bones and stock in a little water. Add the spices and lemon juice, cover and poach in the oven for 20 minutes. Remove from oven, strain liquor from fish fillets, discard herbs and keep fish fillets warm.

Melt the butter in a saucepan, add the flour and cook gently for 2–3 minutes. Remove from heat, add the strained fish stock and blend until smooth. Return to the heat and cook until thick and creamy. Stir in cream and add remaining prawns, adjust seasoning and pour over hot fish fillets. Garnish with parsley sprigs.

Index